COLLINS

CARE
—— & ——
REPAIR OF

ANTIQUES
& COLLECTABLES

COLLINS

CARE
&
REPAIR OF

ANTIQUES
& COLLECTABLES

ALBERT JACKSON & DAVID DAY

HarperCollinsPublishers

**COLLINS
CARE & REPAIR
OF ANTIQUES &
COLLECTABLES**
was created exclusively for
HarperCollins Publishers by
Inklink

**Conceived, edited
and designed by**
Albert Jackson, David Day
and Simon Jennings
trading as Inklink.

Text
Albert Jackson
David Day

Design and art direction
Simon Jennings

Text editor
Peter Leek

Illustration
Robin Harris

Studio photography
Ben Jennings

Index and proofreading
Mary Morton

For HarperCollins
Editorial Director
Cathy Gosling

**Text set in Bembo and
Caslon Openface**
by Inklink, London

Jacket Design
Design: Simon Jennings
Photographs: Ben Jennings
Illustrations: Robin Harris

Colour origination by
Colourscan, Singapore

Printed and bound
by Graficas Estella,
Spain

First published in 1998
by HarperCollins Publishers,
London

ISBN 0-00-413316-1

**The CIP catalogue record
for this book is available
from the British Library**

Copyright © 1998
HarperCollins Publishers

Consultants

The authors are grateful to the following consultants for their contributions and assistance.

PAPER COLLECTABLES

Anthony Cross
Warwick Leadlay Gallery,
Greenwich, London
Elizabeth Howard
Bookbinder
Sydenham, London

CERAMICS

Carmen Villacampa
Ceramics restorer
Badgers End, Dorset

TEXTILES

Alexandra Seth-Smith
Textile conservator
Blackheath, London

PLASTICS

John Morgan
Author of
Conservation of Plastics
published by Conservation
Unit of the Museums and
Galleries Commission and the
Plastics Historical Society

TECHNICAL CONSULTANT CONSERVATION MATERIALS
John Lawson
Picreator Enterprises Ltd.,
Hendon, London

Additional information supplied by

A. Bell & Co. Ltd.,
Kingsthorpe,
Northampton
Ciba Polymers,
Duxford,
Cambridge
Cray Pharmaceuticals,
Eltham,
London
ICI Acrylics,
Darwen,
Lancashire
La Ronka,
Hockley,
Birmingham
Percy Reboul,
Plastics Historical Society,
London
Sapphire Products Ltd.,
Nechells, Birmingham
H.S. Walsh and Sons,
Beckenham, Kent

Additional photography

©**EWA** (Elizabeth Whiting
& Associates), pages 45, 81,
90, 128, 129. **Paul Chave**,
pages 80 bottom right, 108.
©**John Morgan**, page 136.
Neil Waving, pages 88, 91
bottom right, 109. **Shona
Wood** page 91 top right.
© Inklink (**Ben Jennings**
Photography) Jacket and
chapter-opener pages 18–19,
34–5, 52–3, 66–7, 82–3,
92–3, 110–11, 130–131.

The authors and producers are indebted to the following who generously loaned antiques and collectables for photography.

Stephen and Jane Bull
Glen Chapman
Unique Collections,
Greenwich, London
Jim and Pat Clark
Jacqueline Day
Julian and Ellen Day
Robin and Shirley Harris
Pauline Jackson
Rose Jennings
**Christine and
Maurice Johnson**
John Morgan
Alexandra Seth-Smith
Warwick Leadlay Gallery
Greenwich, London

The authors and producers are grateful to the following companies who loaned their products and materials as reference and samples for photography

Chintex
Stove-Enamelling Glaze
Chintex International
Wraxall, Bristol, Avon

Renaissance
Metal De-corroder
Renaissance
Microcrystalline Wax Polish
Vulpex liquid soap
Picreator Enterprises Ltd.
Hendon, London

Badger Airbrush
Richard Kohnstam Ltd.
Hemel Hempstead,
Hertfordshire

CONTENTS

CONTENTS

INTRODUCTION

TO DETERMINE WHAT MAKES SOMETHING DESIRABLE and therefore collectable is difficult, if not impossible. People acquire objects for all manner of subjective reasons, and what one collector judges to be a sound investment another may consider an utter waste of money. You can always rely on criteria such as scarcity and condition – and a famous name stamped on the base of a piece of china or signed at the bottom of a picture may be a mark of value, provided that it's genuine. However, you have only to visit a few antique shops and markets to realize that a large proportion of the trade has moved away from what has traditionally been regarded as collectable.

There's no doubt that television programmes have had a profound effect on people's attitude toward collecting antiques. By focusing on spectacular 'finds' that have netted their delighted owners a small fortune, television has persuaded the average person that it is worth hanging on to heirlooms in case they turn out to be priceless antiques. As a result, fewer items are now making their way onto the market and prices have become inflated. Good pieces are snapped up as soon as they appear, and the apparent scarcity drives prices up still further. With fewer traditional antiques to meet the demand, the trade has inevitably been opening up more abundant seams, drawing out a wealth of items that not long ago would have been rejected by serious collectors. Whereas at one time an object had to be at least 100 years old to be classed as an antique, nowadays the average dealer's stock includes items made in the 1940s and 1950s, or even the 1960s, and it would appear that almost anything has its price.

Far from being a negative trend, the wider availability and respect for what might be termed 'recent antiques' merely serves to widen the opportunities for collectors and amateur restorers. Although rare and valuable antiques have deliberately been excluded, this book covers the widest possible range of collectables from Victorian times to the 1960s; and to make information as accessible and relevant as possible, we have chosen to devote each chapter to a particular material, such as wood, metal or glass, rather than to specific objects such as antique clocks or paintings. Consequently, you can look up appropriate techniques and use them for restoring similar pieces from practically any era.

There is a body of opinion that believes amateurs should never be encouraged to restore antiques, for fear that they may do irreparable harm. When it comes to valuable or fragile antiques, we heartily concur. Nevertheless, we take the view that a great many amateurs who are extremely skilful with their hands often simply lack relevant advice and the necessary information in order to make competent repairs to everyday collectables. This book aims to supply that advice and information, gleaned from informed collectors and practising restorers and conservators.

BUYING ANTIQUES AND COLLECTABLES

For some collectors the excitement of finding a real 'gem' is almost as important as acquiring the piece itself, and discovering a piece that has eluded them for years may assuage pangs of guilt at having paid a little too much for it. In order to maintain that level of pleasure and excitement, a collection has to grow – and finding ready and reliable sources of supply is crucial to the process of building up a collection.

Nobody can advise you what to collect – you are either drawn to it or you're not – but when looking around for things that could be of interest, you might consider opting for items that are plentiful and therefore relatively cheap, rather than try to compete with collectors who have been active in well-explored fields for years. This doesn't necessarily mean you have to go in for an area of collecting that is obscure or miss out on types of antique that are popular – but it does involve doing some research, so you can back your own judgement as to whether something is worth collecting, rather than having to rely on catalogues or makers' names.

In any case, most people who are engrossed in their hobby find that research becomes absorbing and highly rewarding. Books and magazines constitute valuable and readily available sources of reference, but nothing can beat the first-hand experience gained by window-shopping and browsing through markets and auction lots where you can handle antiques and examine them at close quarters. In no time you begin to get a feel for what is available, and whether you are likely to find enough items in restorable condition.

BUYING FROM DEALERS

Whenever possible, any collector prefers to buy items in perfect condition, provided the price is within reason – but the ability to clean up and restore damaged antiques is a distinct advantage, especially as even minor flaws reduce the asking price considerably.

Not all dealers stock damaged pieces, but frequenting a variety of dealers, ranging from top-class establishments to back-street junk shops, gives you a wider choice and also enables you to compare the difference in price between damaged pieces and those in perfect condition.

Get to know dealers who specialize in the kinds of antiques that interest you. You are unlikely to find bargains, but you will pay a fair going rate as the dealer knows the market intimately. Moreover, specialist dealers are invariably knowledgeable about their subject and are usually willing to share that knowledge with you – though it helps if you buy something from them from time to time!

Print dealers and small galleries are often a good source of restorable items. The best-quality material is usually mounted for framing, or for display in the shop; but the majority of dealers also have folders full of torn and stained prints and other works of art, which they may be willing to sell cheaply rather than pay someone to restore them.

Book prices vary considerably from dealer to dealer. There are far too many subjects for a general dealer to keep track of, so there are frequently bargains to be had. Second-hand books can stay on a dealer's shelves for months, or even years – and a bookseller may be happy to do a deal with you, provided he or she did not have to pay too much for it in the first place.

Junk shops that stock anything and everything are always worth a visit, but you have to be prepared to trawl through a lot of second-grade material to find the odd gem. Many of these dealers specialize in house clearance, and most of the good stuff is hived off to auction.

It pays to visit your favourite dealers on a regular basis. You will, of course, see the same stock over and over again, but your persistence will be rewarded when you spot something special that has just come in and can snap it up before anyone else sees it. Also, dealers soon recognize regular customers and are usually willing to reserve items of particular interest. By frequenting a number of outlets, you will have your finger on the pulse and may be in a position to spot a change in the market – certain items becoming rarer, higher prices being asked for items that were once commonplace – and take advantage of your knowledge to pick up a few bargains.

Most dealers are prepared to haggle. Indeed, some of them anticipate it by setting their prices at a slightly inflated level. A 5 to 10 per cent reduction is not unusual, but depends on what the dealer had to pay for the item. So when he or she tells you that a lower price is not possible, accept it graciously – after all, dealers have to make a living. You will not usually get a reduction for credit-card transactions (except perhaps on expensive items), because the dealer has to pay a premium for the service. Most dealers will accept a cheque if you can guarantee it – but cash is usually preferable, especially for cheaper items or if you are haggling for a reduction.

ANTIQUE MARKETS

Antique markets are mostly weekly events where dealers set up their stalls in the open air or halls or club rooms, but there are also permanent or semi-permanent markets in premises such as large warehouses and converted mills. The better markets are often supported by dealers who run antique shops during the week but bring a different stock to the market, where the lower overheads make for keener prices.

There is very little pressure to buy at markets, giving you plenty of opportunity for browsing, comparing prices and examining items at your leisure. Whatever it is you are looking for, you can be sure there is a stall somewhere that has at least a few items of interest. Antique markets are an especially good source of unusual inexpensive jewellery, simply because it is portable. There are dealers who specialize in precious metals and gemstones, but the majority carry a wide selection of jewellery made from amber, coral, ivory and other semi-precious materials. You may also come across collectable pieces made from early plastics.

PRIVATE SALE

You can often find interesting antiques by combing newspaper advertisements or going to private garage sales. In these circumstances, it pays to have a little experience and to be sure of your facts. A private seller may have a highly exaggerated idea of an item's importance and value, perhaps inspired by a similar but rarer item seen on television. However, it may not be appreciated if you start airing your knowledge – so it's usually best to politely decline to purchase and leave it at that.

Boot sales are similar to buying privately. For a modest sum any individual can rent a pitch for the day and sell anything from cut-price foodstuffs to genuine antiques. If you attempt to return something that does not come up to expectation, you may not get much satisfaction, as few of the vendors are likely to be professional dealers.

AUCTIONS

If you are serious about buying and restoring antiques and collectables, keep an eye open for auctions being held in your home town or within easy striking distance. They are usually advertised in the local papers, and the larger or more important ones may be listed or advertised in specialist magazines.

Auctions are sometimes worth visiting even when you don't intend to buy. Specialized auctions can be particularly exciting when prices soar because two or more collectors are after a rare piece. However, at many auctions all sorts of items are up for sale, from furniture to pictures. Job lots are a useful feature of general auctions, where you can buy a box of china, books or records – almost anything – for a fraction of what you would pay if you bought the individual items from a dealer. Auctions are just the place to buy good-quality items at a reasonable price and for picking up exceptional bargains – especially if you are prepared to restore them yourself, since any dealer bidding against you has to allow for the cost of restoration on top of what you are prepared to pay.

Try to visit the saleroom on viewing day (usually the day before the auction). If you wait until the day of the sale, you may not have time to inspect the items carefully – and, as most lots are sold 'as seen', it is your responsibility to spot any defects. Carry a small torch and a magnifying glass, and a notebook in which you can jot down any distinguishing features or marks that you want to check before the sale – another reason for viewing early.

Buy an auction catalogue, giving details of the sale and the price that each lot is expected to reach. Make sure you know whether the figures are estimates or reserve prices, as that may affect the way you bid. If an item does not reach its reserve price, it will be withdrawn from the sale; on the other hand, auction lots often go for prices well below their estimated value.

Check the catalogue carefully for additional charges. Auctions used to charge vendor's commission only, but nowadays it is common to charge a buyer's premium too, usually 10 per cent of the hammer price. It is important to take that into account when deciding what you want to pay for a piece. Also, remember to allow for any relevant tax on top of a successful bid.

Catalogue descriptions are brief and may give very few details about age and provenance. They are often no more than statements of opinion and carry no guarantee of authenticity. You have to know your stuff if you don't want to walk home with a pile of junk – if you have done the relevant research, you will have an advantage over less knowledgeable collectors.

On the day of the sale, mark your catalogue with the top price you are prepared to pay and stick to it. If the bidding intensifies, you may be sorely tempted to keep going, and it is all to easy to pay more than you can afford in the heat of the moment. Don't be too disappointed if you fail to acquire the one piece you had your eye on. This will happen frequently, and just because someone else is prepared to pay more does not necessarily mean the piece is worth it. It is always possible that the successful bidder did not spot the defects you noticed the day before.

The bidding itself couldn't be simpler. The auctioneer makes the running, suggesting the opening bid and then asking for higher bids in simple increments. All you have to do is signify your willingness to pay the asking price by raising your catalogue or nodding your head. Don't be deterred by the prospect of having some unwanted item knocked down to you because of an inadvertent gesture. In real life this doesn't happen. In fact, if you haven't entered the bidding at an early stage, you may have to attract the auctioneer's attention by waving your catalogue or calling out your bid, because he or she will be concentrating on those who seem most intent on outbidding each other. If you have been successful, to secure your purchase you usually need to call out your name, though some auction houses give you a number with which to identify yourself. The catalogue will give you all the information you need about what forms of payment are acceptable and when you can collect your lots.

HEIRLOOMS

If you are fortunate enough to have acquired antiques or collectables through inheritance, have them valued by an expert before attempting any restoration work yourself.

CHECKING FOR FAULTS

Once you show genuine interest in a piece, a reputable dealer will invariably point out any defects and will no doubt have priced the piece accordingly. However, not all dealers are so scrupulous and, as we have seen, a great many auctioneers do not consider it their responsibility to draw your attention to damaged items. In any case, it pays to train your eye, not only to spot faults and blemishes but also to assess whether you will be able to restore a piece yourself or will need professional assistance.

Knowing what to look for will help you over the first hurdle, but only experience can teach you when to invest in expert restoration rather than do the work yourself. Throughout this book you will find specific advice on when to consult experts – but if ever you are in any doubt, consult a trained conservator or restorer. On the other hand, you may take the view that antiques are bound to show their age and that you are happy to live with the inevitable imperfections. This may be the wisest course of all, provided you take precautions to prevent further deterioration.

The following is a check list of the kinds of faults you can expect to find, depending on the material from which an antique is made and the care with which it has been handled and stored in the past. No such list can ever be comprehensive, but it will help you detect the most obvious defects – and perhaps avoid the worst pitfalls.

BOOKS AND PERIODICALS

Ideally when buying books, you are looking for reasonably clean copies with intact bindings. You can't always get books wrapped in their original dust jackets, though that would be a bonus.

It is not a good idea to buy books with torn spines or loose covers unless they are worth the additional cost of professional rebinding. However, you may be able to spruce up dirty or faded book covers yourself, though there is little you can do about heavily stained covers or warped boards.

Flick through a book to check that all the illustrations and photographic plates are in place. If individual plates are loose, they can be pasted back into a book without too much trouble.

At the same time, look out for signs of insect infestation. Woodworm, for example, have been known to migrate from bookshelves and burrow their way right through a book. This sort of damage is impossible to rectify.

It is probably best to reject books or periodicals with badly stained pages, although you can usually remove light soiling. Torn pages and endpapers can be repaired successfully in a number of ways.

PRINTS AND PICTURES

The restoration of oil paintings and other works of art in colour should be left to a professional. It is all too easy to destroy or damage a valuable picture if you are not sufficiently experienced to identify the medium correctly and then decide on the appropriate course of action. It is therefore wisest to concentrate your efforts on inexpensive black-and-white prints or drawings made in pencil or waterproof ink.

Don't be put off by soiled or stained prints. If necessary, they can be washed in water or a mild solution of bleach. Similarly, crumpled or torn artwork can be repaired but, since it will never be perfect again, the purchase price should be very reasonable.

Collectables made from metals are frequently sold in a dirty and corroded state.
Sometimes this is because the dealer simply does not have the time to keep on
polishing them, but the more likely reason is that an experienced dealer knows
that some collectors prefer old metalware to exhibit the dull patina of age and
cleaning the stock might deter potential customers. However, it is usually very
easy to polish tarnished metals if that is the way you like them.

The one exception may be steel or iron, as they rust when exposed to damp
conditions. It is possible to clean and stabilize rusting metal, but if the damage is
severe it can only be disguised by filling and painting, which may be
detrimental to the value of the piece.

Examine plated metalware for signs of wear. The plating on high points is
often polished away, exposing the base metal. It is possible to have pieces
replated, but that more or less destroys their value as antiques. Before buying
chromed collectables, look for signs of blistering, where corroded base metal is
pushing the plating off the surface.

Dents are not too difficult to remove from soft metals, but steer clear of
deeply creased or folded metal because the damage is likely to be permanent.

Broken metalware can be difficult to assess. A lot depends on how
experienced you are at simple metalworking. Depending on the type of metal
and the way a piece was made, it may be possible to solder or rivet loose
components or open seams. But leave welding to an expert. Some breaks can
be mended with glue or discreet mechanical fixings.

It cannot be emphasized enough that you should have antique jewellery valued
by an expert before deciding to work on it yourself.

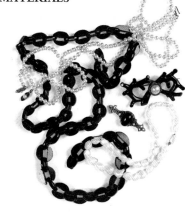

Check that there are no loose or missing stones; and examine pins, clasps
and other fastenings to make sure they are sound and in good working order.
You can generally repair damaged fastenings, using little more than a pair of
padded pliers.

Before buying a necklace, make sure it is strung on strong thread that is not
about to break, although restringing is a viable option. If you buy loose beads
or pearls, make sure they are even in size, shape and colour, and that there are
enough of them to make up a necklace of a reasonable length.

Always examine items made from coral, amber, jet and similar semi-precious
materials for signs of previous restoration, and to ensure there are no obvious
chips or deep scratches.

Bone and ivory were frequently used to make handles for cutlery, manicure
sets and sewing equipment. If this type of handle works loose, it can be cleaned
up and reglued.

China and pottery are easily damaged, so look at a piece from all angles to spot
chipped rims and cracks. Hairline cracks can be difficult to detect unless they
are dirty. If you hold porcelain up to the light, you may have a better chance of
noticing a crack. And if you stand the piece in the palm of your hand and tap it
gently with your fingernail, the porcelain will ring if it is sound.

Mending cracks and chips is relatively easy. Even reassembling broken china
is not too difficult once you have practised the appropriate techniques, but it

takes real dexterity and some artistic ability to replace missing components such as cup handles or a hand on a porcelain figure.

Crazed glaze is something most collectors accept, provided it has not become ingrained with dirt. Given time, it is possible to soak out most ingrained soiling and other stains.

Try to detect old repairs, for two reasons. In the first place, a restored piece should cost you less than one in perfect condition; and, secondly, if you wash a restored piece in hot water it may well disintegrate. You can't miss old riveted repairs, but rivets can prove tricky to remove if you find that you need to make a more satisfactory repair.

Surface decoration may be worn away in patches – often because plates, cups and saucers and other tableware have been stacked carelessly or have been washed in a dishwasher. It is never easy to restore worn decoration. Either decide to live with it or practise on something less desirable until you have developed the necessary skills to restore it.

GLASSWARE It is practically impossible to make invisible repairs to broken glassware. The best you can expect to achieve is a sound and safe repair; but it won't stand up to close scrutiny, nor can you expect to put the item back into service.

Examine glass decanters for old wine stains and white water marks, as they can be difficult to remove. Also, look carefully to make sure that the stopper matches the style and decoration of the decanter.

Coloured-glass windows – leaded lights – are rather specialized antiques. Except for hand-painted panels, leaded lights have little appeal as collectables; but they make attractive glazing, either *in situ*, as originally intended, or hung in front of clear-glass windows. Check old leaded lights for broken or buckled leadwork and for cracked or missing quarries (the individual pieces of coloured or textured glass). They are all repairable, but only by a skilled restorer. On the other hand, it is quite easy to fill the gaps around loose quarries, to stop them rattling, and to clean up dirty glass and leadwork.

You will often come across old mirrors that are 'fogged' or are speckled with small brown stains. These defects are the result of moisture penetrating the silvered backing. There is nothing you can do to rectify these faults except to have affected mirrors stripped and resilvered by a specialist – which tends to detract from the value of genuine antiques.

WOOD When it comes to wooden collectables, it is very often the surface finish that is damaged rather than the wood itself. White water stains and other surface blemishes can be disfiguring – but they are rarely impossible to rectify, although occasionally you may find that you have to resort to stripping and refinishing the whole piece.

Dents, splits and deep burn marks require more work, because you need to treat the wood itself; but unless the damage is very severe, you can generally make a passable repair.

Veneered pieces are especially vulnerable. Glance across a veneered surface to check there are no blisters that will need flattening, and inspect the edges of any veneered panel to see if the veneer is chipped or lifting. Check, too, to see if there is any loose or missing marquetry or inlay.

Always be on the lookout for signs of recent woodworm. A mass of small clean holes and pale dust are signs of recent activity. There is no reason why you should not buy a wormed piece provided it is basically sound, but it is imperative that the infestation is treated early before it spreads to other items made from wood.

TEXTILES

Antique textiles constitute a vast field of collectables that need careful preservation – including old clothes, which many people enjoy wearing. The best advice is to do as little as possible, except for repairs that will prevent further deterioration. As you probably don't want to be seen wearing tatty clothes, examine potential purchases for signs of deterioration, especially in those areas that receive the most wear, such as collars, cuffs and sleeve elbows. Unless you are buying the garments for a collection of historical costume, it is probably best to look for wearable items in better condition.

Check also that all the necessary fastenings and buttons are present and securely attached.

Restoring antique textiles demands slightly different techniques from those normally used for mending modern textiles. It is vital that the methods you use do not put additional strain on what may be weakened fabrics. Holes and tears can be patched successfully, but don't take on the restoration of very fragile or large-scale textiles.

In some cases it is possible to wash or dry-clean soiled textiles. But some old stains – especially perspiration stains – cannot be removed, even by experts.

Usually it is best to reject textiles that show signs of moth infestation. Unless the dealer can guarantee that the textile has been treated professionally, it is not worth the risk of introducing infestation to your collection.

CARPETS AND RUGS

Since carpets and rugs are generally used as floorcoverings, one expects to see signs of legitimate wear and tear. Apart from minor repairs to worn side cords and fringes, there is not much an amateur can safely do to restore a worn carpet or rug. So, if you detect holes, splits or missing fringes, you need to agree on a price that allows for the cost of professional restoration. If you come across a rug that appears to have been folded for some time, examine it carefully to make sure the fibres have not been damaged along the crease lines.

PLASTICS

Not all antique plastics have the same characteristics. Some are brittle and are more likely to crack or shatter. Others will bend without breaking, but may exhibit stress marks along the crease. Again, some plastics are more susceptible to fading than others, and some are more easily scuffed or scratched. Accurate identification is the key – and it will pay to study the chart on page 137, so that you are aware of the most likely defects when hunting for plastic collectables.

POTENTIAL ENEMIES

With the exception of fire, the greatest risks to anything made from paper are damp and high humidity. Moisture not only causes actual physical damage in the form of warping and cockling, it can encourage mould growth and staining. Dampness can also attract insects that feed on organic glues and paper. Generally, a dry but relatively cool environment suits paper products best. With too much heat, paper becomes brittle.

It is also important to protect paper from airborne dust and pollution. Fine dust gets absorbed into the paper, and larger gritty particles act like an abrasive. Even more harmful are invisible pollutants: industrial emissions and traffic fumes can attack and discolour paper.

Long-term exposure to ultraviolet light is detrimental, too. Daylight, the main source of ultraviolet radiation, causes colour pigments to fade and eventually makes the paper disintegrate.

Careless handling and inappropriate storage are perhaps the most common causes of physical damage, especially to items that were considered worthless until somebody started collecting them.

Although it is possible to do a great deal to arrest the deterioration of paper collectables that have suffered in the past, the best possible course is to protect them from adverse conditions. Advice on storage and mounting will be found throughout this chapter.

PAPER COLLECTABLES

The considerations that determine whether a piece of paper is collectable, and therefore worth preserving, have little to do with the material itself. Indeed, two very similar pieces of paper can command vastly different sums of money, depending on what has been applied to them and by whom. A drawing or engraving may have artistic merit to commend it. Another scrap of paper may owe its survival to sentimental attachment; or the fact that it is a charming and colourful piece of ephemera may have saved it from being discarded. Documents and photographs are frequently prized for the information they contain or because of their association with a famous personality. Clearly, although conservation aims to preserve the paper itself, the real objective is to ensure the survival of what is on it.

To a large extent this is likely to colour your approach to conservation. It is important, for example, to decide whether legibility and access to information are more important than aesthetic considerations. And most people would prefer to live with a stained picture, rather than risk losing the image itself.

There are three golden rules. Be clear about your objectives; make sure you know what medium you are dealing with; and proceed with caution. If you are in any doubt, seek the advice of an expert before tackling restoration yourself.

CLEANING PICTURES

The true value of a watercolour, drawing or print may be measured in money, artistic merit, rarity, age, or personal association with a place or person – but what matters more to you as a restorer is whether you can successfully improve its condition or appearance. Old pictures, like all antiques, have a quality that develops with age. Slight discolouring of the paper, stains and muted colours are all clues to a picture's provenance, and can add considerably to its character. Without them, you might just as well hang a reproduction on the wall – so hesitate for a moment and ask yourself whether cleaning will enhance the picture or may in some way detract from its appearance.

Your next decision is whether you can safely undertake the work yourself. This will largely depend on how much the picture is worth and on what medium has been used to create it. Valuable pictures in need of restoration should always be handed over to an expert, as should fragile drawings in chalk, pastel or charcoal. You are on fairly safe ground with black-and-white prints, provided you are sure they are not photographic reproductions; but obtain expert advice before doing anything to coloured artwork. Don't abrade pencil, and never wash ink drawings unless an expert has assured you that the ink is waterproof. Finally, don't attempt to restore artwork on very thin or delicate paper.

Dry methods
Before resorting to more drastic measures, always try erasing blemishes in case they are merely on the surface of the paper. Overall treatment with document cleaner (see right) will increase the contrast of an ink drawing or print, but if you are left with stubborn marks or dirty patches try removing them with a pencil eraser (see page 29). You may be able to pick off tiny specks with the point of a sharp knife, but take care not to pluck the surface of the paper. Use of document cleaner or a pencil eraser is safe for most types of artwork – but not for pencil drawings.

Using document cleaner
Document cleaner – powdered eraser – is ideal for cleaning grubby artwork. Its action is so gentle that it can be used safely on hand-coloured prints and watercolours, provided you do not rub too hard; but never be tempted to use document cleaner on pencil drawings. Available from bookbinders' suppliers, it comes in an open-weave bag that you squeeze to distribute the powder onto the paper.

To avoid rubbing dirt into the paper, brush surface dust off the artwork with a soft brush. Holding the picture firmly on a non-slippery table top, sprinkle document cleaner onto the surface and gently rub the bag over the soiled paper with overlapping circular strokes. Take care to avoid tearing or creasing the paper as you approach the edges.

Washing pictures
If dry methods are not successful, you could try washing the picture in cold water. Even if it does not entirely eradicate ugly staining, washing will at least have the advantage of drawing out natural acidic impurities, which eventually destroy old paper.

The process is usually safe for black-and-white prints, but don't soak coloured pictures or drawings made with water-soluble inks. The same goes for any picture signed with ink, but you will find that pencil signatures are usually impervious to washing in water.

Distilled water – or clean tap water – should remove the majority of stains, or at least reduce them to an acceptable level. Adding a little salt to the water may help to draw out blood and wine stains, but remember to rinse the picture thoroughly in fresh water. Don't use hot water, as it tends to fix stains permanently.

Until you become experienced at washing pictures, don't attempt to soak large prints in water – they become heavy and difficult to handle. The same is true of badly damaged pictures, which have a tendency to disintegrate when they become wet. Washing thin and delicate paper is also a task best left to an expert.

Foxing
Small brown spots known as 'foxing' are caused by spores growing on damp paper. If necessary, foxing can be dispelled by immersing the print in a mild bleach solution.

Equipping yourself

You can improvise to a certain extent, but you will find washing and drying prints easier – and more efficient – if you avail yourself of a few specialized products. They are sold by bookbinders' or conservators' suppliers, most of whom offer a mail-order service.

Archival support fabric, made from non-woven polyester, enables you to handle wet paper safely and facilitates air drying by natural circulation. For this you also need a drying rack, made by stapling fibreglass 'fly-mesh' netting across a softwood frame. If this purpose-made netting is unobtainable, try using fine plastic netting from a garden centre.

You can wash paper in any large plastic bowl or bath, but it pays to buy a flat tray designed for washing photographic prints. Make sure the tray is large enough to allow your prints to lie flat under water.

1 Immersing the print in water
Cut a piece of support fabric to fit the bottom of the tray, making sure there is enough to support the print on all sides. Fill the tray with cold water, and gradually immerse the supported print by sliding it beneath the surface from one end.

2 Rinsing regularly
After about 20 minutes, carefully remove the support fabric and print, refill the tray with fresh water and reintroduce the print. Repeat the process four or five times, with 20 minute intervals.

3 Leaving the print to dry
After the fifth rinse (or sooner if you get a satisfactory result), take the print and its support out of the water and lay them on your drying rack. At this stage it doesn't matter if the print does not dry completely flat, because you will probably need to size the paper anyway (see page 22). If you prefer, wait until the print is almost dry, then press it flat between two sheets of clean blotting paper, using a warm iron.

Water staining
Accidental soaking draws dirt into the fibres of the paper. Prints in this condition often benefit from washing in cold distilled water.

Bleaching prints

If after being washed in water your print still exhibits a disfiguring stain, you could try immersing it in a weak solution of bleach. However, bleaching artwork is a controversial subject. Some authorities maintain that amateur restorers should never attempt bleaching – indeed some would suggest that bleaching is not to be recommended under any circumstances, because of the possible long-term effects on paper fibres. To be safe, it's best only to bleach inexpensive black-and-white prints; anything else should be tackled by an expert. Ensure that the paper is thoroughly soaked in cold water before you put it into a bleach solution.

Make a solution of bleach and water in the same tray you use for washing artwork. The professional restorer would mix 4 teaspoons of Chloramine T in half a litre (1 pint) of cold distilled water. This bleach is available from specialist suppliers only. Alternatively, use a household 'sterilizing fluid' – a mild bleaching agent and antiseptic used, among other things, to sterilize babies' bottles. Mix sterilizing fluid with 4 parts water.

1 Bleaching the print
Wearing close-fitting vinyl gloves, lower the print, backed with archival support fabric, into the bleach solution. Keep an eye on the print and, as soon as the stain disappears, lift the print out carefully, pour away the bleach and refill the tray with fresh water.

2 Rinsing the print
Leave the print to soak for 20 minutes before replenishing the water. Repeat the process five times, as described for washing artworks, then leave the print on a drying rack to dry naturally.

Damaged prints
Torn prints can be repaired with starch paste or document-repair tape. Badly damaged artworks may need relining (see page 24).

SIZING PAPER

Paper that has been bleached and soaked in water is relatively weak and benefits from a coat of size. Make a suitable size by mixing 10gms (half an ounce) of ordinary gelatine in half a litre (1 pint) of water.

Applying the size
Lay the washed and dried print face down on a clean sheet of paper. Coat the paper generously with size, using a wide, soft brush to cover the print evenly. Blot off excess size and leave the print on your drying rack to dry naturally.

REPAIRING PICTURES

Repairing creased or torn pictures is relatively straightforward with modern conservation-grade materials, provided the damage is slight. It is vital to ensure that the image on the paper will not be harmed or obscured by the processes.

Flattening creased drawings and prints

Once paper has acquired a distinct fold, it can be difficult if not impossible to rectify. However, damping and pressing a pencil drawing or a black-and-white print might minimize the effect. Don't try this with coloured work or ink drawings unless you have been assured that the medium is entirely waterproof. Similarly, avoid spraying any picture that was previously glued to a backing board, in case the water reactivates the adhesive.

Spraying and pressing the paper

Lay the creased picture face down on a clean sheet of damp blotting paper, and moisten the back of the print or drawing with a plant spray filled with distilled water. Moisten a second sheet of blotting paper and lay it on top of the print.

Place all three sheets of paper between two stiff boards, and weight them down with heavy books. Alternatively, put the boards in a press until the paper has dried.

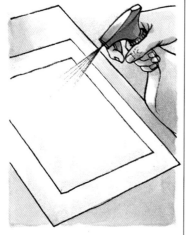

Eliminating a scored line or indentation

A sharp edge or point pressed into paper leaves a deep impression. If the image itself has been scored, seek the advice of a professional restorer. But if the indentation is across the border of the picture, you can use an artist's brush to paint hot water along the scored line.

Let the water soak in for a few minutes to allow the paper fibres to swell, then lay blotting paper over the blemish and rub it down with a bookbinder's bone folder or tacking iron (see page 31).

Repairing torn artwork

The methods for repairing torn artwork are the same for any graphic image drawn or printed on paper – but, since recommended archival paste is made with water, the usual restrictions apply to artwork made with water-soluble materials. Nevertheless, so long as the damage does not extend across the image itself, careful repair work should leave the picture unharmed.

Similarly, although conservation-grade adhesive tapes and tissue make excellent reinforcements when applied to the back of a picture, it is not advisable to apply them across the image itself, even though these materials are practically invisible when rubbed down.

Mending a simple tear

More often than not, a tear in relatively thick paper has overlapping feathered edges, which are easy to rejoin with starch paste. Use a specialized bookbinder's paste or buy conservation-grade wallpaper paste. Both types of paste are reversible, and are guaranteed not to stain the paper or promote mould growth.

Use a pointed artist's brush to apply paste sparingly to one feathered edge, then bring both torn edges together. Wipe off any excess paste with a clean paper tissue, cover the repair with silicone-coated release paper, and rub it down with a bone folder.

Reinforcing a repair

A glued repair should be sufficiently strong without any further reinforcement. But if the overlap is minimal or the paper was cut, leaving no feathered edges at all, apply a special self-adhesive paper tape to the back of the picture. Archival document-repair tape is made with reversible acrylic adhesive which, unlike the glues used for ordinary stationery tapes, will not deteriorate and stain the paper. When rubbed down with a bone folder, document-repair tape is almost invisible – and you can buy a slightly yellow tape that approximates the colour of old paper.

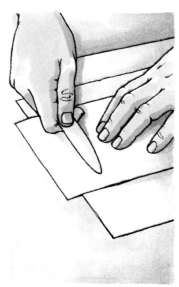

Relining a badly damaged print

Simply regluing the torn edges may not be sufficient to repair a print that has been ripped in half. A more professional approach is to reline the picture by pasting handmade Japanese tissue paper to the back. It is not easy to achieve perfect results, but considering that a badly damaged print is probably worth very little, you are not risking a great deal.

Nevertheless, it is advisable to have the picture valued before you proceed.

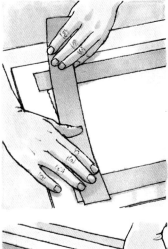

1 Preparing the tissue

Tear or cut the Japanese tissue paper 50mm (2in) larger than your print on all four sides. Lay the paper onto a sheet of glass and moisten it with a plant spray. Tape the moist paper to the glass with gummed brown-paper tape and leave it to dry.

2 Pasting the print

Brush starch paste onto the back of each half of the print and lay them onto the tissue paper, carefully aligning the torn edges. Lay a sheet of silicone-coated release paper over the print and gently rub it down, using a soft-cloth pad. Peel off the release paper and leave the print to dry.

3 Trimming the picture

Once the print and tissue paper are dry, trim around the taped edges with a very sharp knife and lift the relined print off the glass.

MOUNTING AND STORING PICTURES

Display and store your collection of pictures within the normal living areas of your home, where it is easy to maintain a relatively dry, clean and stable environment. But don't hang framed pictures in direct sunlight, or above a direct source of heat such as a radiator or fireplace.

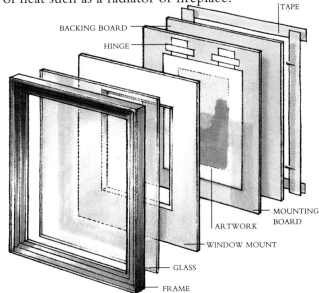

TAPE
BACKING BOARD
HINGE
MOUNTING BOARD
ARTWORK
WINDOW MOUNT
GLASS
FRAME

Framing pictures

Ready-made picture frames are rarely suitable for displaying antique prints, drawings or watercolour paintings. There is no guarantee that they are made from conservation-grade materials – and inexpensive frameless versions, comprising a sheet of glass clipped to a stiff backing board, offer little protection from dust and airborne pollution.

Whether you make your own frames or order them from a professional framer, it pays to ensure that only acid-free boards and paper are used to mount your pictures. Conservation-grade materials are widely available from art-material shops and conservators' suppliers

The style of frame is a matter of personal taste. But if you are in doubt, choose a slim, simple moulding for the frame and off-white or cream-coloured mounting board that will not detract from your picture.

All artworks on paper should be framed behind glass (non-reflective picture glass is an option, but not essential). Some collectors prefer to use transparent polycarbonate or acrylic sheeting. These materials are marginally safer than glass and can be treated to protect your pictures from ultraviolet light. However, plastic glazing can acquire a static charge that makes them unsuitable for chalk, pastel or charcoal drawings.

Thin double-sided hardboard, sealed with acrylic varnish, supports the picture from behind and protects it from damage.

Cutting mounts

Most prints, drawings and watercolours are sandwiched between two sheets of mounting board, one with a window cut through it to display the artwork (it also maintains a space between the glass and the picture). When measuring the window mount, allow a generous border all round the image. By convention, a relatively wide border beneath the picture makes for a visually balanced mount. The window itself, which is usually cut with bevelled edges, should allow enough room for the picture to 'breathe' and should never conceal a plate mark (the impression left in the paper during the printing process) or the artist's signature.

Mounting the picture

The picture should never be pasted to a mounting board directly. Instead, hang it from Japanese-paper hinges attached with starch paste (see page 23). Paste another strip of paper across each hinge to reinforce it.

Inserting the backing board

Once you have assembled the frame, along with the glazing and mounted picture, secure the backing board in the frame rabbet with non-rusting brads or metal 'points'. Finally, seal the gap around the backing board with gummed brown-paper tape to protect the picture from dust and insects.

Storing pictures in folders or boxes

If you are a serious collector of prints or drawings, it will no doubt be impossible to display your entire collection in wall-hung picture frames. In which case, store your pictures in shallow boxes made from acid-free cardboard. These purpose-made boxes, available in a wide range of sizes, have metal-reinforced corners and a front flap that drops down to provide easy access to the contents once the lid is removed. Either make a simple paper folder for each picture or interleave them with acid-free tissue paper.

CONSERVING OLD PHOTOGRAPHS

Like other prints on paper, photographs need protection from light, dust and physical damage. In addition, the chemical composition of the photographic emulsion makes them particularly susceptible to pollution and fluctuating levels of temperature and humidity.

As a general rule, keep your photographs in a relatively cool environment, free from dust and moisture. Try to store them away from exterior walls and painted or varnished surfaces that might exude harmful fumes. Never use a damp cellar or a dry, dusty attic for storing photographs.

Safe storage

The traditional photograph album is still one of the best ways to store old photographic prints. It enables you to view your collection easily and quickly without having to touch any of the photographs, and will prevent them fading as a result of exposure to light. It is possible to buy albums that are made entirely from conservation-grade materials. You may also want to purchase transparent polyester corner mounts that are chemically stable and guaranteed not to cause long-term deterioration of the emulsion.

Storing individual photographs

An album may not be suitable for storing an extensive collection, nor if you want to be able to compare or check information printed or written on the reverse.

You can wrap one or two photographs in acid-free tissue and slip them into a strong envelope, but do make sure the envelope is not made with glued seams that might react with the photographic emulsion.

File a larger collection in strong archival-quality cardboard boxes, with each photograph enclosed in an acid-free, non-alkaline paper wallet – or, better still, in a transparent polyester sleeve that allows you to handle the print without touching its delicate surface. All these materials are available by mail-order from conservators' suppliers.

Displaying photographs

Display old photographic prints in wall-hung frames, in a similar way to other artworks printed on paper (see page 24). However, be particularly choosy about the boards you select for your mounts. Most so-called acid-free card is 'buffered' with an alkaline substance to prevent acid contamination. These are perfectly adequate for most archival purposes, but research suggests that buffered boards in close contact with photographs may be harmful in the long run. Unbuffered materials should therefore be chosen in preference.

Reproducing old photographs

One way to avoid possible harm to a fragile or rare photograph is to make a copy – the original can then be stored safely and the reproduction displayed without risk. Even badly creased, stained or faded photographs can be improved and enhanced without having to retouch the original. Many high-street photographers act as agents for this highly specialized service.

Mending torn photos

You can make a passable repair to a torn photograph using starch paste (see page 23). It won't repair cracked or flaked emulsion, but gluing the torn paper may prevent further damage to the photograph. Paste the torn edges together, as described on page 23. If necessary, reinforce the back of the print by pasting a narrow strip of Japanese tissue paper over the repair; alternatively, use archival document-repair tape.

Restoring photographs

If you have rare or valuable photographs that need restoring, have the work done by an expert able to identify with certainty the exact base and chemical process that was used for a particular print. However, you can clean and repair your own family photos – which may not be valuable in monetary terms but are worth preserving for future generations to enjoy.

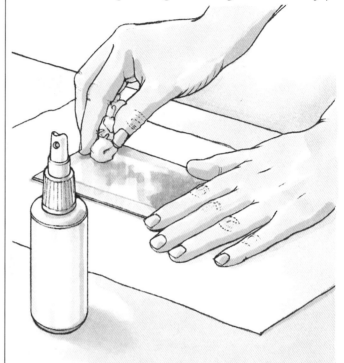

Cleaning prints

Cleaning an old print with water is likely to cause the emulsion to swell. However, you can remove fingerprints, mould and some ink marks from the surface of old photographs with a cleaning fluid available from conservators' suppliers. Spray the fluid onto a clean lint-free cloth and gently rub the print using circular strokes. The fluid should dry instantly, without leaving a residue.

RESTORING BOOKS

Being made largely from paper, books suffer from exposure to damp, dust and insects and the effects of physical abuse. But because the paper is bound between cloth- or leather-covered boards, the restoration techniques already outlined for pictures and printed ephemera have to be adapted to suit the peculiar construction of books.

How books are made

Books are printed on large sheets of paper that are folded and trimmed to make sections of leaves, which are sewn together to make the basic book block. The spine – the sewn edge of the block – is reinforced with a strip of open-weave fabric, known as mull, and sometimes with transverse strips of cloth tape. Decorative headbands are sometimes glued across the top and bottom of the spine.

The mull and tapes form hinges or 'joints' between the block and the book cover, which is made by covering thick strawboard or millboard with cloth or thin leather. Relatively thick endpapers, glued to the inside of the cover, conceal the joints and form a flyleaf at the front and back of the book.

Many books are wrapped in a decorative paper dust jacket. You should always attempt to preserve a book's dust jacket, whatever its condition, since it is invariably of value to collectors (see page 32).

Restoring books yourself

A lot of restoration strays into the realms of bookbinding, a highly skilled activity that demands specialist knowledge and practice to perfect. Old books in very poor condition are therefore likely to require the services of a professional. This is especially true of volumes with decorative or fragile leather bindings, and always consult an expert about the restoration of rare or valuable books. However, cleaning and making minor repairs to ordinary second-hand books is well within the capabilities of the amateur who is willing to purchase a few specialized tools and materials. You can buy all the equipment you need from any bookbinders' or conservators' supplier.

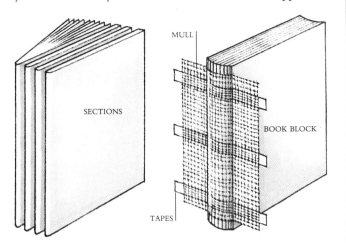

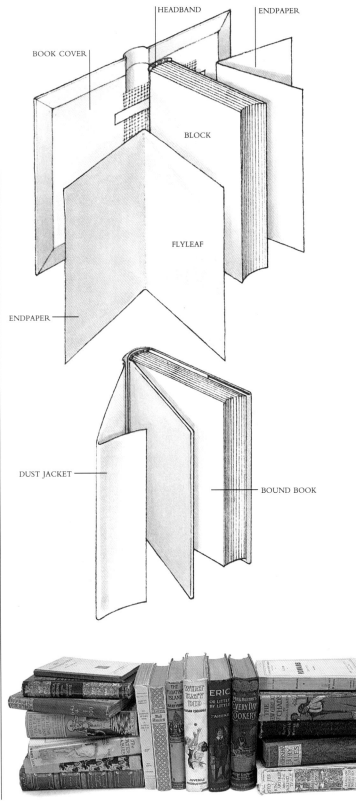

Cleaning books

It is important to dust your books regularly. As well as reducing the risk of dust particles making their way down between the leaves, it provides an opportunity to inspect your collection for signs of mildew and harmful insects. To avoid the possibility of introducing spores and insect eggs, dust recent acquisitions thoroughly before putting them on your bookshelves. Temporarily remove loose dust jackets before dusting books.

Cleaning cloth book covers

Although dusting removes loose surface dirt, it will do nothing for grubby covers that have lost the protection of their dust jackets. Cleaning the cloth cover will not restore the book to pristine condition, but it can spruce up a dowdy copy by reviving the colour of the cloth. Unlike water (which may damage metallic-foil blocking), a proprietary book-cloth cleaner is safe to use on any cloth-bound book.

1 Applying book-cloth cleaner
Take a little cleaner on a ball of cotton wool and rub it across the cover, including the spine, using overlapping circular strokes. Turn the cotton ball as it becomes dirty.

2 Buffing the cover
Leave the cover to dry for a few minutes, then buff the cloth with a clean soft-bristle shoe brush. This should give the cover a nice even colour.

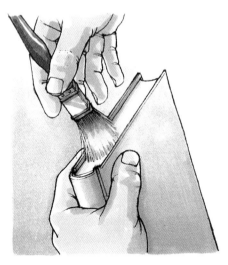

Dusting a book
Holding the book tightly closed between your forefinger and thumb, use a soft-bristle paintbrush to dust off the head, brushing from the spine outwards. Wear a gauze face mask when cleaning very dusty books.

Dealing with mildew

If you discover mildew growing on the cover of one of your books, check your collection for other affected copies and put them aside to dry out thoroughly. This is best achieved by standing the books upright with their leaves fanned open in a dry, well-ventilated area. Check your bookshelves to discover and rectify the source of the damp that caused the contamination.

Once a book is perfectly dry, take it outside to brush off the powdery deposits. There is very little you can do yourself to correct warped boards or stained cloth covers – but if the damp conditions have left the cover looking dull, though basically clean, then you can revive its appearance with white microcrystalline wax polish. The same process will restore some of the colour to a faded spine.

Applying microcrystalline wax
Dip a ball of cotton wool in the wax then, after dabbing the pad on a piece of scrap paper to remove excess polish, rub the wax sparingly onto the book cover, using circular strokes to spread it evenly. Take care not to smear wax onto the pages. A few minutes later, buff the cover with a soft-bristle shoe brush or lint-free cloth pad.

Cleaning endpapers and flyleaves

You will often find the flyleaf or title page of a book inscribed with the names of previous owners, dedications, dates and occasionally the signature of the author or illustrator. Some people attempt to erase such marks if the names are not well known, but it is a pity to lose these reminders of a book's past history. It makes better sense to remove only unsightly scrawls and dirty patches that truly spoil the book's appearance.

Using document cleaner

Rubbing with document cleaner (see page 20) is the safest method for cleaning grubby endpapers – but take care if you want to preserve anything written in pencil. Document cleaner can be safely used on printed and coated endpapers provided you do not rub the paper vigorously.

Support the open book to avoid straining the joint, and rub gently outwards from the centre of the flyleaf to make sure you don't crease or tear the paper. Carefully brush the powdered debris from the book before you close it.

Stained and foxed books

Books that have been stored in damp conditions or subjected to flooding are often disfigured by water stains or exhibit brown speckling known as foxing. Both can be eradicated by washing or bleaching the paper (see pages 21–2) – but since neither method is practicable with a bound book, it is probably best not to buy stained or foxed copies unless you are prepared to put up with them in that condition.

Erasing underlining

Though not impossible, it can be difficult to erase pencilled notes or underlining from the pages of a book, since the paper is likely to have taken an impression. Don't buy books that have been underlined with ink or felt-tip markers – such marks cannot be removed without damaging the paper.

Using pencil erasers

Try using a good-quality soft eraser made from white vinyl. In addition to the usual small blocks, these are available as refills that fit a retractable stylus – ideal when you need greater accuracy. Alternatively, use a soft putty-like eraser that you can knead into whatever shape is convenient and reshape as it becomes dirty.

Whatever type of eraser you choose, support the open book and rub with short straight strokes from the spine towards the edge of each leaf (don't use circular or reciprocal strokes, which could crease the paper) and work diligently to avoid erasing print. Stippling with a softened putty eraser will often remove dirty patches, without having to rub the surface.

Cleaning plates

Document cleaner will remove dirt and smears from the surface of illustrative plates (avoid using erasers that tend to leave streaks on shiny coated paper). Take extra care when cleaning plates – you may find that they are just 'tipped in', or lightly glued into the book.

Repairing damaged books

Don't be deterred from buying a book just because it has broken joints or the endpapers are missing. This type of repair is a professional bookbinder's stock in trade, and you may find that the cost of restoring the book is perfectly affordable. You certainly don't need specialist skills to remedy dog-eared pages or to replace a loose frontispiece or mend a torn page – all that is required is care and patience, and you can practise on books of little worth before you tackle something you care about.

You will have to judge for yourself whether it is advisable to clean the paper before repairing it. You don't want to trap dirt under a strip of pasted tissue or tape, but there is always a risk that you could make the damage worse by rubbing the paper with document cleaner or an eraser. The condition of each book will suggest the best course of action. It is generally accepted that it is best to leave cleaning the cover until last.

Some of the techniques suggested for repairing books can also be used for restoring magazines, comic books and other printed ephemera.

Flattening folded corners
Some readers have the habit of folding the corner of a leaf to mark their place. Also, the pages of books printed on thin paper often have dog-eared corners as a result of careless handling or storage.

Rubbing with a bone folder
Open out all the affected corners, using the tip of a bookbinder's bone folder. Place a piece of cardboard under the damaged leaf and lay a strip of thin paper on top of it, then flatten each corner in turn by rubbing down the crease with the folder. The crease will always show, but the leaf will at least remain flat.

Inserting a loose plate
A scrupulous dealer may have already made a note of missing plates. If not, before buying a book, look at the list of illustrations in the front matter. Alternatively, the number of illustrations may be printed on the title page.

Loose plates are not a problem. They can be reinserted easily – and this is something you should do as soon as possible, before their edges become scuffed and dirty. If you are not sure where a plate should be inserted, check whether its intended location is printed in the margin.

Individual plates, including the frontispiece, are usually tipped in (glued along one edge) and simply require repasting. With more modern books, pairs of plates tend to be wrapped around sewn sections – in which case you need to tip both plates back into the book to make an effective repair. Use a reversible conservation-grade PVA adhesive, available from bookbinders' suppliers.

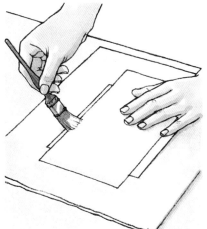

1 Applying adhesive
Lay the loose plate face down on a sheet of clean white paper. Mask the back of the plate with another sheet of paper, leaving a thin strip exposed along the plate's inner edge. Paint the adhesive sparingly onto the plate's exposed edge, brushing outwards from the mask.

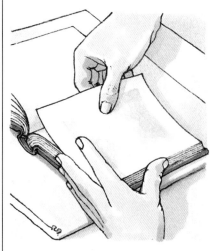

2 Inserting the plate
With the book open, use a finger and thumb to align the corner of the plate, while holding the glued edge away from the leaf below. Carefully rub down the glued edge, then lay a strip of silicone-coated release paper into the hinge and close the book.
Leave the release paper in place until the adhesive has set.

Repairing torn leaves and endpapers

There are several options for repairing torn books. Your choice will depend on whether the repair needs reinforcing and whether you are willing to buy specialized equipment.

A water-based paste is cheap and simple to use, and may be all that is required to make an acceptable repair. Applying conservation-grade self-adhesive tape makes for a stronger repair and is practically invisible, even on printed pages.

Heat-set tissue is a good alternative to self-adhesive tape and can be torn to whatever shape is required to cover irregular tears. However, you need a special electrically heated tacking iron to set the adhesive.

Pasting torn paper

A simple overlapping torn edge can be repaired with paste (see page 23). Sandwich the repaired page between two sheets of silicone-coated release paper, close the book and leave the paste to dry.

A properly glued repair should not require reinforcing, but if the book is to be used frequently or the repair is vulnerable in any way, it pays to cover the repair on at least one side with document-repair tape (see page 23) or tissue paper.

Using document-repair tape

Wash your hands before handling adhesive tape. Choose the tape that most resembles the colour of the page, and tear it into a narrow strip with feathered edges. Apply the strip of tape to the page, lay a piece of paper on top and rub it down with a bone folder to exclude trapped air. Place a piece of card beneath the repair, then use a steel rule and knife to trim excess tape flush with the edge of the leaf.

Reinforcing with heat-set tissue

Coated tissue paper, with a heat-setting acrylic adhesive on one side, produces a repair that is barely discernible. The adhesive is protected with a carrier sheet, which should not be removed until you are ready to make the repair.

Tear the tissue to follow roughly the shape of the damage and lay a piece of the carrier sheet on top. Rub down the tissue with the broad tip of a hot tacking iron.

If you want to make a repair without pasting the edges first, begin by laying a protective sheet of paper on the damaged leaf, then flatten the fibres along the torn edges with a bone folder. If you don't do this, a slight ridge may be apparent underneath the tissue. Apply tissue to both sides of the leaf.

Reinforcing weak or torn folds

Illustrated books sometimes have fold-out maps and diagrams that are in need of attention, especially if the paper on which they are printed has become brittle with age.

Reinforce a weak fold by applying document-repair tape (see left) or a strip of heat-set tissue (see above) to the back of the illustration.

If a diagram has torn into several pieces, it is best to reline it with handmade Japanese paper (see page 24) – but only if you can be sure that water is not going to harm the printed surface. You can make a similar repair with heat-set tissue, though a heated press is needed in order to set a large area.

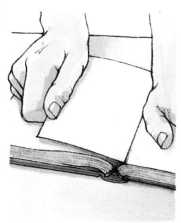

Removing a tipped-in diagram

Folded diagrams or maps are invariably tipped into old books. If you intend to reline a torn diagram, you need to remove any pieces that remain pasted in, so you can make an effective repair. Holding down the adjacent page with the flat of your hand, peel back the glued edge with a straight pull. Once you have repaired the diagram, paste it in place, as described for inserting a loose plate (see opposite).

Repairing a cracked hinge

The joint between cover and book block is an obvious weak point. Endpapers are therefore often the first to show signs of wear along the hinge line. Provided the mull and reinforcing tapes are still intact, you can restore the appearance of a joint by regluing the ragged edges where the endpaper has cracked. Timely action can save printed or illustrated endpapers, which become difficult to repair once the entire joint fails.

1 Applying glue to the crack
Carefully peel back the torn edges, so you can brush out any dust that may have penetrated the crack. With a narrow pointed paintbrush, paint conservation-grade paste sparingly into the crack, making sure that the paper is evenly coated.

2 Closing the crack
Use the blade of a blunt table knife to lift and press the cracked hinge back into place, aligning the torn edges exactly. Wrap a barely damp, lint-free rag around your finger and press down the glued edges, while wiping off any smears of paste.

3 Pressing the book
Fold a strip of silicone-coated release paper and place it into the joint, then close the book and rub down the joint with your finger. Place the book between two stiff boards, aligning them with the joints to avoid crushing the spine. Place a heavy weight on top and leave the glue to set overnight.

Protecting dust jackets

Dust jackets are especially vulnerable to damage, which is probably why so many second-hand books are sold without them. If you are lucky enough to acquire a copy with an intact jacket, it pays to protect it with a transparent sleeve that will keep it clean and prevent further deterioration.

For rare books you may want to buy purpose-made jacket protectors, but as an inexpensive alternative for less valuable copies you can adapt the bags used by florists for wrapping bouquets of flowers. Before sleeving the jacket, smooth out any creases and realign torn edges. The sleeve or bag may hold a slightly damaged jacket together without further treatment, but repair a badly torn jacket with heat-set tissue (see page 31) or document-repair tape (see page 23) before sleeving it.

1 Making the sleeve
Cut the sealed end off the bag to make an open-ended sleeve that is approximately 25mm (1in) shorter than the overall width of the dust jacket. Slip the jacket into the sleeve, until it fits snugly against one folded edge and projects an equal amount from each end of the sleeve.

2 Folding the sleeve over the jacket
Place the sleeve and jacket face down on a table. Align a long, straight rule with the top edge of the dust jacket and, while holding the rule down firmly, fold the sleeve over the jacket. Remove the rule and rub down the crease.

3 Wrapping the book
To ensure that the sleeved jacket fits snugly, begin by wrapping it around the spine of the book, then place the book flat on a table with the spine facing you. Open the book and fold in one jacket flap. Close the book, turn it over and fold in the other flap.

MAGAZINES AND PERIODICALS

Since they lack the protection of cover boards, magazines, comic books and other periodicals are extremely vulnerable to physical damage. You can clean them and repair torn or creased pages using methods similar to those described for bound books. What sets most periodicals apart from sewn books is that the sections are held together with metal staples; consequently if they have been stored in damp or humid conditions, the staples are likely to have rusted, staining the surrounding paper. If the paper is becoming fragile, then your only option is to remove the rusted staples and sew the periodical with linen bookbinding thread.

Three-hole sewing
There is little you can do about rust staining; but if the paper has torn around the staples, close up the hole and reinforce it with a torn strip of document-repair tape before sewing.

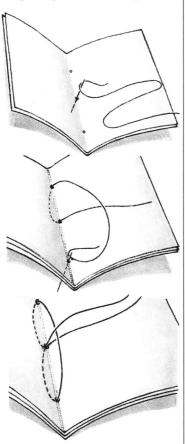

1 Starting at the centre
Punch a small hole through the dead centre of the hinge, and two more equidistant from the centre. Start by pushing a threaded needle through the central hole from inside the magazine.

2 Passing back through
Pass the needle back through the top hole and, skipping over the central hole, pass the needle out through the bottom hole.

3 Tying off
Now pass the needle back through the central hole, cutting off the thread to leave two long tails on the inside of the magazine. Tie these in a knot, enclosing the length of thread running down the centre of the hinge. Finally, trim off the tails.

Storing magazines and comic books
Keep individual magazines and comic books in transparent sleeves made from polyester or polyethylene. File your sleeved collection in acid-free cardboard boxes.

GOLD AND SILVER

Although they have many other uses, gold and silver are primarily associated with fine jewellery. The quality and colour of these metals – whether used on their own, or together, or combined with other precious or semi-precious materials – make any item made from them special. Gold is very soft and therefore easily damaged (how easily depends on its purity). Silver is harder, though still relatively soft compared with most other metals. Items made of solid gold or silver are expensive because of their metal content. To reduce cost and weight, some pieces are made hollow. Also as a cheaper alternative, gold and silver are often plated onto metals of lesser value. Rolled gold and silver, fused to a base metal and rolled into a thin sheet, can usually be identified by their lack of markings and relatively light weight. Electroplate (see page 38), which has a thin chemically bonded film of precious metal, was developed in the mid nineteenth century and largely superseded rolled gold and silver.

GOLD STANDARDS AND MARKS

For commercial use gold is alloyed with other metals (usually silver or copper) to improve its strength or modify its colour. The quality of gold is represented by its carat value, which is the proportion by weight of pure gold to the alloyed metal(s). Pure gold is 24 carat. The current gold standards are 22, 18, 14 and 9 carat, although 15 and 12 carat were also produced in the past. Genuine British pieces are stamped with a carat number, maker's mark, assay-office mark (hallmark) and a date letter. In North America carat is spelled with a 'k' – which, together with the maker's mark, helps to identify items of North American origin.

METALS

The practical and aesthetic properties of metalware are much appreciated, but when it comes to anything more than light cleaning, metal is mostly viewed as a difficult and unsympathetic material to be worked only by specialists. Yet down-at-heel objects made from this versatile material can be usefully restored with basic craft skills.

Metals or their compounds are extracted from ores or metal-bearing minerals and then either processed into various grades of a single metal or combined with other metals to form a range of alloys that have different properties.

It is often difficult to identify metals very precisely, but it is usually possible to recognize the general type by its colour, weight and hardness. The object itself is also a clue, as the characteristics and value of the various metals tend to lend themselves to particular uses.

Colour is generally the most useful guide, although this will vary according to whether the surface is polished, tarnished or corroded.

GOLD AND SILVER JEWELLERY

Have valuable precious-metal jewellery cleaned and maintained by a professional jeweller. Gold does not tarnish, and plain pieces need little more than a rub with a soft cloth or chamois leather to keep them bright. Remove light tarnish from silver with a proprietary long-term silver cloth.

Dirt in the form of grease from soap or make-up can mar the appearance of a piece that is intricately shaped or set with gemstones, making further cleaning necessary.

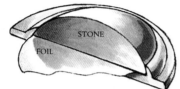

CLOSED SETTING

OPEN SETTING

Checking the setting

If the piece is set with stones, examine it closely. Gemstones may be held in a closed or an open setting. With a closed setting, the stone is enclosed in a recess formed in the mount. Sometimes a foil backing is placed behind the stone to enhance colour and brightness. This type of setting should not be exposed to moisture, nor should enamelled pieces.

An open mount gives access to the back of the stone, which makes cleaning easier. Provided the stone is not porous, simply wash it in warm soapy water.

Remove finger rings, or wear rubber gloves to protect them, when doing domestic washing.

Using a dip cleaner

Use a commercial dip to clean small or intricately detailed jewellery that is not affected by moisture. Dips are available from jewellers in a range of types for cleaning gold, silver and gemstones. Use a separate dip for each type of material.

Following the maker's instructions, place one item at a time in the dip solution for the prescribed duration (usually not more than a minute). Remove the piece from the dip and gently brush the surface with the small soft brush provided as part of the kit. Rinse thoroughly in clean water, then dry with a soft cotton cloth or chamois leather.

Cleaning open settings

Clean large pieces of open-backed jewellery – such as a brooch – with a solution of mild washing-up liquid. For better-quality jewellery use conservator's liquid soap and warm water (1 part soap in 10 parts water), plus a few drops of ammonia. Use a plastic bowl placed on the sink drainer. Do not work over the sink itself, as you risk losing pieces down the drain. Remove the dirt with an old toothbrush, then rinse in clean warm water and dry by blotting with a soft cotton cloth or paper kitchen towel.

Cleaning closed settings

Since trapped moisture could damage the setting, use methylated spirit or specialist isopropyl alcohol, instead of soap and water, to loosen grease and dirt. Apply the spirit carefully with a cotton bud, and wipe off the residue with clean buds as you go. For light soiling, use dip-cleaner fluid applied with a cotton bud. When dry, buff carefully with a chamois leather.

Chains

Wearing a gold or silver chain regularly will keep it bright. However, it may be necessary to remove grease and dirt from time to time. For solid chains, use a dip or wash them in liquid soap and warm water or a mild solution of washing-up liquid.

Do not immerse a hollow chain in liquid: if it is made from plated metal, trapped moisture may cause corrosion. Instead, pin each end to a softboard panel covered with cotton cloth. Remove the dirt from the outstretched chain with a soft brush dampened with dip or mild soap solution. If need be, turn the chain over. Blot moisture and loosened dirt from the chain with absorbent tissue, then polish with a soft cloth.

Simple repairs

In most cases repairs to precious-metal jewellery are best done by a jeweller, and it is not advisable to attempt them yourself. However, there are some very basic repairs, requiring only simple tools, that you can undertake yourself on items that will not be unduly harmed. (See also pages 54–7.)

Storing jewellery
Keep regularly used gold or silver jewellery in a cloth-lined tray that has separate compartments, or in individual padded-velvet boxes or fabric pouches available from jewellers and specialist suppliers. This ensures that the soft metal will not get scratched or dented and prevents necklaces and bracelets becoming tangled. For long-term storage, wrap each piece in acid-free tissue. Rolling chains in the tissue makes them easier to handle. Keep jewellery in a stable environment away from excessive heat.

Chain rings
Jump rings are used to form a closed loop at one end of a chain and to link a clasp or bolt ring at the other. Both jump rings and bolt rings can be damaged by wear or distorted by force. If they are beyond repair, you can buy gold or silver replacements in various sizes.

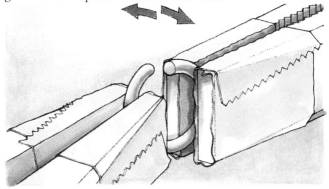

Fitting a jump ring
Always open a jump ring by twisting the butting ends sideways, using two pairs of small pliers. Wrap the jaws of the pliers with adhesive tape to prevent them marking the metal. Open the ring no more than is necessary to loop it into position, then close it by twisting the ends back together.

Replacing a bolt ring
Bolt rings are fitted in a similar way to jump rings. They are available in a range of sizes and come with an attached open or closed ring for fitting to the chain.

Loose finger rings
Loose finger rings all too easily get lost. If you prefer not to have a loose ring permanently resized by a jeweller, you can reduce the internal diameter by fitting a ring clip.

Buy a clip that fits the width of the ring band and simply spring it into place.

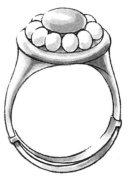

SILVERWARE

Silver is an important commercial metal that has been used for a wide range of domestic wares. Generations of silversmiths have produced beautiful pieces, which by virtue of their craftsmanship and use of material have become desirable to collectors. And yet it is still possible to discover silver items such as matchstick cases, cups and pots that have not been recognized for what they are. For, if left unpolished, silver will tarnish in the presence of a sulphurous atmosphere, turning first yellow then dark blue or black. To confirm that a piece is silver, look for the maker's mark stamped in the metal.

English silver is the easiest to identify, as a system for standardizing the quality was introduced in the thirteenth century, consisting of a series of marks giving details of the assay office, quality, date and maker. These marks may be accompanied by a number indicating the parts of silver per thousand. Continental Europe and North America did not adopt such formal regulations for the control of the silver trade, though town and maker's marks were used and can be a useful guide. However, silver marks are not always clear or genuine – and careful analysis, aided by reference books, is advisable.

Sheffield plate
Invented in 1742, Sheffield plate is a thin rolled-sheet material, consisting of silver fused to a copper backing. One or both sides may be plated. The edges were often lapped with silver or covered with silver wire, sometimes making identification difficult. Worked like solid silver, it was used for a range of flat and hollow domestic silverware. Although Sheffield plate was not generally marked, nineteenth-century items may have simulated silver marks.

Electroplated silver
The electroplating process, introduced in 1820, enabled cheap silverware to be produced by electrolytically depositing a thin film of silver onto preformed base-metal pieces. Electroplated nickel silver (EPNS) is often used for cutlery and other items of tableware; an alloy of nickel, copper and zinc, it is sometimes referred to as German silver. Britannia metal (EPBM) – an alloy of tin and antimony – is also used.

Silver gilt
Silver electroplated with a thin covering of gold is known as silver gilt. It is used for plating hollowware, jewellery and decorative items. It should be treated as electroplated silver.

Cleaning silverware

Polish silver as little as possible, as overenthusiastic cleaning can cause more harm than not cleaning the metal at all. Hollowware, such as teapots and jugs, and tall narrow pieces such as candlesticks, can be distorted or broken by rough handling, while repeated polishing of silver-plated pieces can wear through the surface and expose the base metal.

Handling silverware
For flatware, such as dishes and salvers, cover the table with a soft cloth to cushion the piece. When polishing hollowware, always support it well. Do not press down on lightly made pieces, nor hold them by their handles or spouts. Instead, cradle the object against you, supporting it from underneath with one hand. Wear an apron and, to prevent tarnishing as a result of fingermarks, wear cotton gloves. Specially treated gloves are available for cleaning and polishing silver.

Washing silverware
Regularly used silver usually needs no more than routine washing to maintain its shine. Tarnished silver should be washed before it is polished, in order to remove any traces of dust or grit that could scratch the surface. Where possible, before cleaning, remove items such as teapot or coffeepot knobs made from other materials. Using a soft cloth, gently wash one piece at a time in a plastic bowl filled with a solution of warm water and liquid soap (see page 36) or mild washing-up liquid. Use a soft brush to get the dirt out of crevices. Rinse in clean warm water and dry immediately with a soft cloth; you can also use a hair dryer for drying intricate pieces. Buff the metal with a proprietary silver cloth.

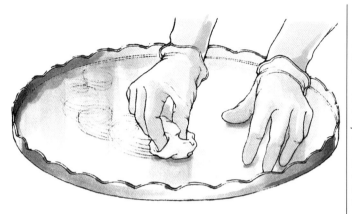

Removing tarnish

There are a number of cleaning products available for polishing silver: impregnated cloths and wadding, silver foams, silver creams and liquid polishes. Choose one that is chemically formulated to give long-term protection – every time a piece is polished some silver is removed, and a long-term polish will avoid the need for frequent cleaning.

Apply the polish with a soft cloth, following the manufacturer's instructions. Work gently in a circular motion, turning the cloth when it becomes dirty; then buff the surface with a clean cloth. To clean decorative work, use a soft brush or cotton buds or wadding. After cleaning, wash the polished metal to remove any traces of cleaner, then dry thoroughly, giving it a final rub with a soft cloth. Take extra care with plated silver, and as an alternative use a silver dip (see below).

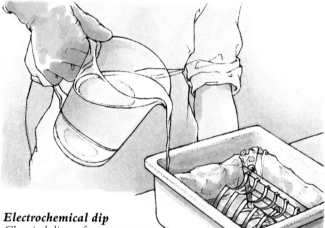

Electrochemical dip

Chemical dips soften or remove tarnish from silver, copper and brass by an electrochemical process. For small items, use a commercial silver dip or swab the piece with the dip solution.

To make your own dip for cleaning large objects, line a plastic bowl or bucket with about 1 metre (3ft) of aluminium kitchen foil. Or use an old aluminium saucepan. Tie a length of string to the piece, and place the silverware in the container in contact with the foil or pan.

Wearing vinyl gloves, make up a solution of 1 cupful of washing soda (sodium carbonate) to 2 litres (3½ pints) of very hot water. Make sufficient to cover the item completely, and pour it carefully into the bowl. A chemical reaction will cause the solution to bubble as the tarnish is removed.

Lift the piece out frequently to monitor progress. When it is clean, remove it from the dip; wash and dry it immediately, and then polish. For very heavy tarnish, it may be necessary to repeat the process.

Another alternative is to use a commercial cleaning plate. This will produce the same electrolytic reaction, but cooking salt is used in the hot water. There is also a tarnish-removing product for silver in the form of a sachet that contains all the materials required – you simply add water.

Do not use a dip for cleaning items that are composed of a mixture of materials – including ones with weighted bases, such as candlesticks – nor treat separate pieces made from different metals in the same dip solution. Strip old lacquer before cleaning (see page 41), and do not use a dip for artificially patinated wares.

Cleaning niello

Niello is a type of silverware decorated with engraved designs filled with a black compound. Particular care is needed when cleaning niello, as the piece will be damaged if the compound is removed. Never use a dip, but lightly clean the surface with a long-term silver polish to reveal the design.

Storing silver

Wrap pieces in acid-free tissue to protect the surface from abrasion and atmospheric pollution. To avoid condensation problems, place them in ventilated polyethylene bags and store in a cool place. Cloth wraps and bags impregnated with tarnish inhibitor are also available for protecting silverware.

COPPER AND BRASS

Polished copper cooking pots and pans, kettles and jelly moulds demand to be displayed around the walls or surfaces of any kitchen. Indeed for most of us copper and brass epitomize the homeliness of old-fashioned country kitchens.

It is surprising that copper should have been used for cooking pots, since it can contaminate foodstuffs that react with it – which is why copper vessels are usually lined with a coating of tin. Nevertheless, it does absorb and hold the heat easily and evenly, and copper pans are still favoured by chefs today.

Unlike copper – which is a pure metal and has a pinkish colour – brass is an alloy of copper and zinc, and its attractive bright-yellow colouring can be mistaken for gold. There are, however, many different types of brass, some of which contain a higher proportion of zinc, as well as other metals such as tin, lead and nickel. Brass has good working and casting properties and considerable strength. It is used for a variety of domestic items, such as lamps, vases, coal scuttles and ornaments, and also for household fittings such as door knobs, finger plates, hinges and locks.

Cleaning copper and brass

Atmospheric pollution will tarnish both copper and brass. Old polished copper takes on an attractive warm-red patina that is best preserved by not overcleaning. Uncared-for copper, on the other hand, tarnishes to a dirty, dull brown, and if exposed to moisture may develop a green coating of verdigris. Such corrosion is sometimes desirable for copper outdoors, as the oxide becomes stable and the weathered appearance looks most attractive. Brass tarnishes to an unattractive dull, greenish brown. Brass is traditionally polished to a bright finish, but looks best when it has mellowed to a rich golden yellow.

Washing the metals
Before polishing copper or brass pieces, first wash them in a solution of warm water and liquid soap (see page 36) or mild washing-up liquid. Use a soft brush for working into mouldings. Rinse thoroughly in clean water, and dry well with a soft cloth.

Polishing
Wearing protective gloves, use an impregnated polishing cloth to polish lightly tarnished copper or brass. Always use a separate cloth for each metal. Treat heavier tarnish with a commercial copper-and-brass cleaner, applying it with a soft cloth and working with a circular motion. Remove the cleaner and polish the surface with a clean, soft cloth.

Dealing with corrosion
Use a chemical dip (see page 39) to soften stubborn tarnish. For local spots, make a paste of cooking salt and white vinegar and apply it to the mark with an artist's bristle brush. Try to avoid runs, as the cleaned brass will turn slightly pink. Rinse off after 10 minutes, and repeat if necessary. Finally, wash and dry the item thoroughly, then polish to restore the colour.

Waxing copper and brass
A simple and effective way to reduce tarnishing and the need for regular polishing is periodically to apply a thin coating of microcrystalline wax, using a soft cloth.

Lacquering metal

You can eliminate the need for harmful regular cleaning of ornamental copper, brass and silverware by applying a clear lacquer. Brush-on and spray-on metal lacquers are available. Lacquers can preserve the finish for many years in normal household conditions. Work in a warm, well-ventilated dust-free room or workshop.

1 Preparing the surface

Polish the metal – but not with a long-term cleaner, as that can affect the bonding of the lacquer. Wash the piece to remove all traces of polish and dry it thoroughly. Wearing cotton gloves, wipe the surface with methylated spirit to remove oily fingermarks.

2 Applying the lacquer

Using a soft, fine brush, apply the lacquer quickly and evenly. Two coats are preferable to one, as there is a tendency for a heavy coating to puddle in mouldings. Turn the piece as you go, working systematically to ensure all surfaces are coated the first time. Leave to harden overnight before applying the second coat.

Spraying lacquer

Lacquers can be thinned and applied to fine detailed work with a spray gun. You can also buy aerosol cans for finishing copper and brass. These are quick to use and avoid brushmark problems, but can produce a heavy spray. Follow the manufacturer's instructions carefully.

Removing lacquer

Worn or missing lacquer creates a patchy appearance. Before the metal can be polished, the old lacquer must be removed. If shellac has been used, remove it with swabs of methylated spirit, or acetone for cellulose lacquers. Use paint stripper if these fail to make an impact, and also for removing other types of lacquer. When cleaning an item made from a mixture of materials, make sure you apply solvents to the appropriate surfaces only. Clean a small area at a time.

ORMOLU

Ornate gold-coloured pieces, such as candelabras, clock cases and fancy metal mounts on the corners of furniture, are likely to be made from gilded cast brass or bronze, known as ormolu (French for ground gold). True ormolu has a thin coating of gold over the base metal, but some examples are simply fine-polished lacquered brass, while others are gilded spelter (see page 44).

Ormolu should not be polished, as it is easy to remove the surface gilding. Wear on the high points of mouldings is acceptable and should not be retouched. Have fine or corroded ormolu restored professionally.

Cleaning ormolu

Clean ormolu with great care. Where possible remove mounts, taking note of their position and fixings. If the gilding is in good condition, it may be possible to clean the surface. For light soiling, remove any dust then clean and protect the surface with an application of microcrystalline wax. For heavier soiling, try gently removing old furniture-wax accretions, using white spirit applied with cotton buds. Follow with a warm solution of conservator's liquid-soap (1 part soap in 10 parts water), to which a few drops of ammonia have been added. Apply the solution with well wrung-out cotton-wool swabs, then wipe with swabs dampened with clean water. Dry thoroughly and buff with a soft cloth. Apply a protective coating of microcrystalline wax.

Fixing a loose handle

Old copper and brass vessels often have handles fixed with copper or brass rivets. Wear can cause the handles to loosen. Should a rivet be missing, buy a matching replacement to fit the hole. Solid rivets are made in copper, brass, aluminium and mild steel. Dome-headed rivets (known as snap-head rivets) are usually fitted, but countersunk or flat-head rivets may also be used. You can buy rivets from metal and tool suppliers, or from specialist suppliers; if you only need one or two, you may be able to obtain them from a local blacksmith.

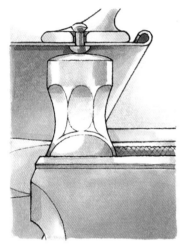

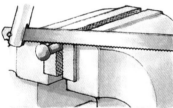

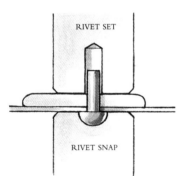

RIVET SET

RIVET SNAP

RIVET SNAP

RIVET SNAP

Tightening rivets
If the rivets are in place and not badly worn, try securing the handle by spreading the rivets in their holes.

Depending on the shape of the vessel, support each rivet on the inside with a metal stake or hammer held in a vice. Make sure the handle is held tight against the pot. Using a ball-peen hammer, strike the rivet to compress it in the hole; then, if need be, use the ball end to re-form the head by carefully tapping it in a circular sequence.

1 Replacing rivets
For a snap-head rivet, cut the length so that one and a half times the diameter of the shank protrudes through the hole. Hold the waste end in a vice and cut the rivet to length with a junior hacksaw.

To form a smooth dome-headed rivet, you will need a rivet set, two rivet snaps and a ball-peen hammer.

2 Fixing the rivet
Place the rivet through the hole from the inside. Support the rivet head in one snap held in a vice. Place the set over the rivet shank and strike it to force the parts together. Remove the set and hit the end of the rivet to spread it.

3 Shaping the rivet
Roughly shape the dome with the ball of the hammer. Then place the second snap over the head of the rivet and hammer it down to produce the final smooth shape.

Removing dents in copper and brass

Light dents in copper and brass vessels caused by normal use can be accepted as part of their period character. However, a large dent in a prominent part can disfigure the form. Have the work carried out by a specialist if the piece is valuable, or if the dent is creased or likely to be difficult to remove.

1 Using a sandbag and mallet
For simple shapes, such as a plain bowl, use a leather sandbag and a wooden bossing mallet, both available from tool suppliers. You can make your own sandbag from sewn canvas filled with silver sand. Form a hollow in the sandbag to support the bowl, and tap out the dent from the inside.

2 Using a stake
Make a wooden stake from a close-grained hardwood such as beech, with the end shaped to a curve slightly tighter than that of the inside of the dented bowl or vessel (this method can be used for other forms, besides bowls). The end of the stake must be smoothly finished. Place the bowl or vessel over the stake and tap out any unevenness on the outside, using a soft-headed mallet.

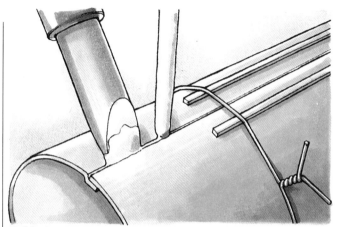

Soldering a seam

Use a large electric soldering iron for making a joint in relatively thin metal, to repair an item such as a copper pot. The larger the 'bit', the more heat it can hold. Heat the iron; when it melts the solder easily, it is ready. Dip the bit in flux to clean it, then apply a little solder to 'tin' the tip. With the components temporarily clamped or wired together, apply the flux to the joint then heat it with the iron. Hold the iron in contact with the seam at one end and apply the solder; at the right heat, it will melt and flow into the joint. Run the iron along the seam, followed by the solder, to form a continuous joint. Avoid using too much solder, as an unsightly excess can be difficult to remove without damage. Allow the metal to cool, then clean off the flux.

Soldering copper and brass

Soldering is a method of joining metals using a molten alloy with a melting point lower than that of the metals to be joined. On cooling, it forms a permanent bond. This process may be divided roughly into two categories, soft soldering and hard soldering. Soft soldering uses a low-melting point alloy of tin and lead that only needs local heat from a soldering iron or blowtorch. It is not particularly strong, but it is simple to use and entails the minimum of equipment. Its silver-grey colour is readily identifiable on old copper wares and tinplate.

Hard soldering – otherwise known as brazing or silver soldering – uses solders that have a high melting point. It produces a strong joint for brass and silverware. The metal has to be at or near red heat; and to generate and maintain such high temperatures, a gas blowtorch and a firebrick hearth are required. Silver solder alloys are available with a range of melting points for assembling complex pieces. Repair work of this kind should be placed with a specialist.

Soft-solder fluxes

Metal that is to be soldered must be clean. Also, a flux has to be applied in order to protect the joint from oxides, since oxides resist solder and would weaken the bond. Two types of flux are commonly used, active and passive. Acid-based active fluxes are corrosive and must be washed off after use. They are more effective for soft-soldering copper, brass, tinplate and steel, as they help to clean the surfaces. Non-corrosive passive fluxes, sold as resin paste or in resin-cored solder wire, are purely protective, so the parts need to be thoroughly cleaned.

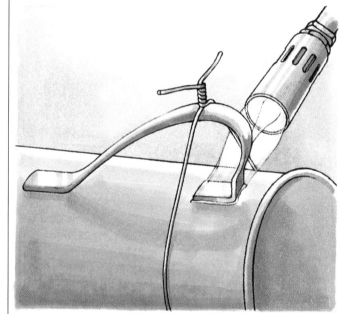

Fixing separate parts

When a component such as a handle becomes detached, it should be possible to refix it with a 'sweated' joint – both parts being first coated with solder. If the faces of the old joint are not well covered, clean the surfaces, apply a flux and recoat or 'tin' them with a thin layer of solder. When they have cooled, apply more flux then position and clamp the parts together. Apply heat with a soldering iron or blowtorch until the solder flows in the joint, then leave to cool. Wash away all traces of flux prior to polishing.

BRONZE

Bronze is a particularly good metal for casting, which is why it is so widely used for statuary and moulded ornaments, intended for indoor or for outdoor use. Bronze is basically an alloy of copper and tin, but its properties and colour can vary with the addition of lead or zinc. Old bronze develops a much-prized, rich-brown patina, which should always be preserved. Some pieces may be artificially coloured to reproduce this effect. When placed outdoors, bronzes develop a greenish-blue patina.

Caring for bronzes

Bronzes should not be overcleaned, as that will ruin their colour. Simply dust the surfaces regularly to prevent the build-up of dirt. Use a soft brush to remove dust from crevices. Never wash bronze unless you are sure it is not patinated spelter (see below), as you run the risk of damaging the colouring. You can wash a piece made entirely from bronze with a liquid-soap solution (see page 36), applying it sparingly with cotton-wool swabs. Alternatively, use a mild washing-up liquid. After washing, dry the piece thoroughly. Treat dull bronzes with microcrystalline wax to clean and revive the surface. Apply it with a soft cloth, then buff it with another clean soft cloth. Indoors, keep bronzes away from damp conditions to prevent corrosion.

Exterior bronzes

Outdoors, bronzes develop a stable greenish patina that needs little attention unless subjected to heavy industrial pollution. To protect the metal, wash the surface with a solution of liquid soap and warm water (see above). Leave to dry, then seal with a thin coating of microcrystalline wax applied with a soft-bristle brush. Rewax from time to time.

Bronze corrosion

Bright-green powdery spots may be an indication of bronze disease caused by a reaction of copper salts within the metal. Clean with metal decorroder, then rinse with clean water, dry thoroughly with a hair dryer and finish with microcrystalline wax. If the problem persists, consult a specialist.

Spelter

Spelter was used in the mid nineteenth century as a cheap substitute for cast-bronze statues and ornaments. An alloy of zinc and lead that has good casting properties, it was either patinated to look like bronze or decoratively painted or gilded. To check whether a bronze-coloured casting is made from spelter, make a small scratch on the underside. If the exposed metal appears silvery, then the casting is not genuine bronze. Clean and maintain spelter the same way as bronze.

PÊCHEUR

PÊCHEUSE

PEWTER

Pewter is perhaps best known in the form of period domestic flatware, tankards and candlesticks, but it also became fashionable in the early twentieth century for Art Nouveau pieces. Old pewter was primarily an alloy of tin and lead, but antimony, copper or bismuth were sometimes used in place of lead. Examples of the finest plate pewter, which contained no lead, may bear an 'X' quality mark. Maker's marks may also be found on early pewter. Britannia metal, developed in the late eighteenth century, was a high-quality form of pewter widely used for silver-plated wares. It looks like silver when polished, but dulls to a light-grey colour. Modern pewter, which is an alloy of tin and antimony, has a tarnish-resistant finish that resembles dull silver.

Caring for pewter

Old pewter generally has a stable dark-grey patina that needs little attention. If it has a high proportion of lead, then the colour is likely to be particularly dark. Handle pewter carefully, as it is a soft metal and so can easily be dented or scratched. Do not use coarse abrasives on old pewter, as they will damage the patina. However, some collectors prefer to keep their pewter brightly polished.

Maintain the condition of pewter by removing dust and buffing occasionally with a soft cloth. Wash soiled wares in a solution of liquid soap in warm water (see page 36), rinse thoroughly and dry with a soft cloth.

Do not store pewter in an atmosphere that contains organic acids – for example, inside an oak cupboard or in boxes constructed from man-made materials containing a high percentage of glue. Wrap individual pieces in acid-free tissue and place them in ventilated plastic bags.

Corrosion on old pewter may cause small lumps to appear. If the condition is not stable, have it treated by a specialist.

Reshaping pewter
Pewter is soft enough to be manipulated by hand. If you have a hollow vessel that has been slightly deformed so it is no longer quite round, squeeze it carefully with both hands to ease it back into shape.

Restoring buckled flatware
For flatware with a lightly buckled rim, work the edge between your fingers and thumbs to straighten it. If you find the metal is too hard to work with your fingers, place the rim on a thick pad of newspaper and gently manipulate it with a wooden seam roller, as used for wallpapering.

METAL TOYS

Until the middle of the nineteenth century the majority of children's toys were simple, locally made playthings. But with the Industrial Revolution and the development of mechanized production, it became possible to mass-produce metal toys at an affordable price. Manufacturers soon discovered that there was a lively demand for representational toys depicting all manner of subjects – including soldiers, animals, boats, trains and automobiles.

Antique toys made of lead or tinplate – or, later, die-cast zinc – have become highly collectable; and examples in good condition can fetch high prices. It is unusual to find an old toy in mint condition, but a well-used plaything showing normal wear and tear is generally preferable to one that has been stripped and restored.

Lead castings
Lead is a very soft and heavy metal that has excellent casting properties. In addition to toy-making, it was used for much larger work, such as garden statues and architectural fittings. When first cast it has a bright silver colour, but this soon oxidizes to a stable light-grey patina, which usually weathers well and needs little attention. Lead is toxic if ingested, so always wash your hands after handling it.

Lead soldiers

At first lead soldiers were cast as simple 'flat' figures. Solid-cast figures, which were more animated in form, then took over, until manufacturers began to produce cheaper hollow-cast models. The soft nature of lead makes it difficult for a toy to remain in perfect shape, and parts easily get bent or broken. However, although lead is very malleable, it is not advisable to try to straighten bent pieces since there is a risk of fracturing the weakened metal. Do not repaint old lead soldiers, as that will considerably reduce their value.

Mending broken parts
It may be possible to refix a broken part of a hollow-cast figure by reinforcing the break with a wooden peg or short piece of solder wire glued into the hollow section. If need be, ream the hole with a drill bit to make it symmetrical. Try the parts for fit, then apply a clear general-purpose glue into the holes, fit the peg and assemble the joint.

Recasting missing parts

Solid-cast soldiers were sometimes made with separate plug-in heads. If the head of a soldier is missing, it may be possible to cast a replica from another head. The replica can then be glued into place and painted with enamel. To make a casting, you will need cold-cure silicone rubber for the mould and low-melt casting alloy for the figure. Various cold-cure moulding rubbers are available from specialist craft suppliers to suit the size and complexity of the moulding. Choose a firm-setting rubber for hand-casting low-melt metals.

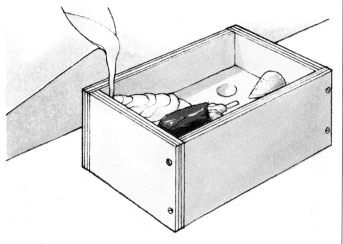

1 Making a two-piece mould

Make a wooden box to contain the rubber mould. Make it a generous size to ensure the sides of the mould are thick. Apply a release agent of thinned petroleum jelly to the inside. Half fill the box with soft clay and press the head of the lead soldier into it so that it is half buried. Also, turn or carve a wooden cone and press it halfway into the clay at one end. This will create a reservoir for the molten metal. Impress cone-shaped indentations into the clay around the head in order to form location pegs. Thoroughly mix the silicone rubber and catalyst together, following the manufacturer's instructions, then fill the mould box and leave the rubber to cure.

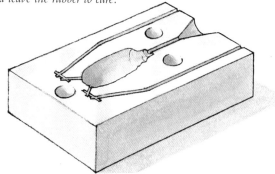

2 Making the second half

Turn the mould box over and carefully remove the clay. Clean the model head, wooden cone and exposed rubber. Apply release agent to the surfaces and fill the second half with rubber as before. When the rubber has cured, remove the box, split the mould and remove the head and cone. Using a scalpel or linocut tool, cut a channel from the reservoir to the head spigot; also cut air vents from the bottom of the moulding to the top of the mould. The vents prevent airlocks forming when the metal is poured.

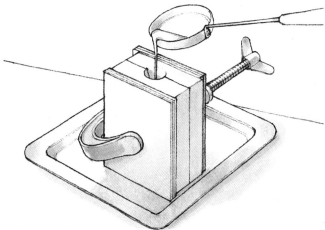

3 Casting the metal

Dust the two halves of the mould with talcum powder, then clamp them together. Choose a suitable casting metal from the range offered by specialist suppliers. An alloy with an extra-low melting point is best for hand casting.

Using a flat-bottomed ladle, melt the metal on a stove. Pour the liquid metal into the mould until full, then leave to cool.

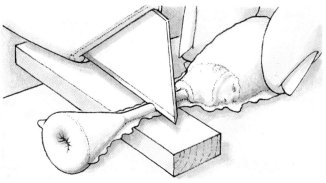

4 Fitting the head

When the moulding has set, remove it and trim off the sprue (waste metal) with a sharp knife. Try the head for fit and trim the neck spigot as required, then glue it into place with a clear general-purpose adhesive. Paint the new head as appropriate.

CASTING METAL SAFELY

* ★Always read and follow the manufacturer's instructions.
* ★Place the mould on a metal tray.
* ★Wear leather gloves and strong protective clothes.
* ★Protect your eyes with goggles.
* ★Wear a face mask.
* ★Do not work near children or animals.
* ★Do not cool hot metal with water.
* ★Wash your hands after handling lead.

TINPLATE

Tinplate is composed of a thin rolled-steel sheet plated on both sides with a thin rust-proofing layer of tin. Tin is a soft, non-toxic durable metal that does not corrode easily but forms a stable light-grey oxide. As a plating material, it is typically used for food canning, as a lining for copper wares and for tinplate used in various lightweight pressings. In solid form, it has been used for domestic flatware and hollowware. It is also widely used as an alloy with other metals.

Tinplate toys
Until Victorian times toys were mostly made from wood, but with the development of tinned steel in the mid nineteenth century manufacturers began to mass-produce lightweight pressed-tinplate toys. These flourished in Germany, America and Britain, with a number of companies producing a variety of tinplate toys, including clockwork horse-drawn carriages, boats, trains and, eventually, automobiles.

Early examples were assembled with solder and painted by hand. An improved method of assembly for mass production featured a series of slots to receive tabs that were bent to lock the parts together. This allowed components to be finished individually before being assembled. Later in the nineteenth century, the introduction of offset lithography enabled toy makers to print detailed designs on the tinplate before it was pressed into shape.

Cleaning tinplate toys
It is best to clean tinplate toys as little as possible, as the surface finish is very thin. Dust them periodically with a soft cloth, or a soft artist's brush for parts that are awkward to get at with a cloth. Provided the tin plating is intact and the decorative finish is sound, you can remove grime with mild washing-up liquid or a warm solution of liquid soap (see page 36), applied with a soft cloth. Take care not to allow water to penetrate inside the toy, and dry the surface thoroughly. To remove greasy marks, wipe the surface with white spirit. Apply a thin coating of microcrystalline wax to protect the finish.

Treating rust
Since the steel is plated with such a thin covering of tin, exposure to atmospheric pollution for long periods is likely to cause the base metal to corrode. Rust is difficult to eliminate successfully, so it is best to place valuable items in the hands of a specialist. If there is light rusting on less treasured pieces, you can try treating the problem yourself.

1 Removing loose rust
Using a miniature power drill fitted with a brass-wire brush, carefully remove the loose rust. Take great care not to damage painted areas. Degrease the surface with white spirit, then wipe dry.

2 Applying rust remover
Brush on a coat of proprietary metal decorroder to remove and arrest the corrosion. Check the surface periodically, and when it is clean carefully wipe off the rust remover with a cloth and clean water. To brighten the metal, rub the surface with a mildly abrasive chrome polish. Wipe the surface and dry it thoroughly, then seal it with a coat of microcrystalline wax. Repainting the toy is likely to reduce its value.

Fixing a broken tab
Metal that is bent will become brittle or work-hardened, and if continuously flexed will eventually break. If one of the tabs holding the parts together has broken off, you can make a replacement. Using tinsnips, cut a strip of tinplate from a suitable can to the required width and length. Clean the faces of the tab and inside the toy, which at this stage may have to be dismantled. Next solder the tab in place, using a passive flux and soft solder (see page 43); or if the heat is likely to damage the painted finish, use an epoxy-resin adhesive to fix it. Finally, assemble the components and fold the tab over.

DIE-CAST ZINC

A light-grey metal with a low melting point, zinc is used as an alloy with copper to produce brass. Alloyed with small quantities of aluminium and magnesium, it is also the main constituent of die-casting alloys. Although in thin sections zinc castings are relatively lightweight and brittle, it reproduces fine detail well and is widely used in the manufacture of model vehicles.

Caring for die-cast toys

The dull-grey colour of zinc alloy is not particularly attractive, and so it is usually finished with paint. Models are frequently found with chipped or worn paintwork, but they should not be repainted or touched up as that can reduce the value to a collector. Place die-cast models in a display cabinet where they are not in contact with one another. Or for long-term storage, keep them in their boxes, if available. Mint-condition models in their original boxes are much sought-after.

Removing dirt
Dust occasionally with a fine brush to keep the surfaces clean. Wash dirty painted surfaces carefully with cotton-wool swabs moistened with soapy water (see page 36). Take care around small projecting details, which can bend or break off. If necessary, use a small brush. Rinse with clean water and dry the surface with a soft cloth or absorbent paper tissue.

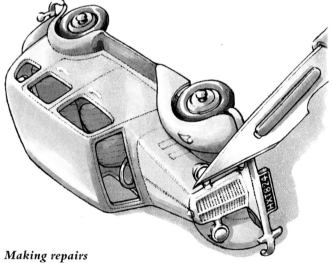

CHROMIUM PLATING

Chromium is easily recognized by its shiny bright-silver colour. It is commonly electroplated onto various metals, including brass and zinc castings. In the 1920s it came into vogue as a finish for furniture, lamps, automobile fittings, art objects and much else.

Chromium provides a tough finish that lasts particularly well on brass. But poorly applied coatings on steel or zinc alloys may result in the underlying metal corroding, causing the plating to blister. Little can be done by hand, other than to treat the surface with a proprietary chrome polish. However, since a chrome finish is meant to have a shiny, bright appearance, it is possible to have items in poor condition chemically stripped and replated by a specialist.

Making repairs
Small-scale details, such as projecting headlamps on models of old cars, are vulnerable to damage. Should a part break off, refix it with an epoxy-resin adhesive or instant-setting cyanoacrylate glue. If using an epoxy adhesive, brace the part while it sets and use a scalpel to trim away exuded adhesive before it has fully cured. The joint won't be as strong as the original metal, so handle the repaired model with care.

IRON AND STEEL

Alloys of iron and carbon form a range of important commercial metals, which are used to produce anything from building structures to industrial and domestic machines, art objects and utilitarian items of all sizes. The types of metal most commonly encountered fall under the headings of wrought iron, cast iron and steel.

Wrought iron is a malleable low-carbon metal, once widely used for handcrafted work. A relatively corrosion-resistant iron, it was used extensively for architectural features such as railings, gates, locks and hinges. Its use declined with the development of cast iron.

Cast iron is a high-carbon metal that has good casting properties. It came to prominence in the nineteenth century, when it was used for the mass production of a wide variety of architectural components and domestic products. It enabled manufacturers to produce highly decorative pieces at a low cost.

Steel is a refined iron alloy made in a range of types that vary according to the materials of which it is composed. Plain carbon steel – or 'mild steel', as it is generally known – is a common form that is easily worked by hand in a similar way to traditional wrought iron.

Identifying iron & steel
When iron and steel corrode, they form a red ferrous oxide generally known as rust. For protection, both metals are usually finished with paint, oil or wax, or plated with another metal. In order to establish the nature of the metal under an opaque finish, test it with a magnet: if the magnet sticks, the metal is an iron-based alloy. To identify the type of metal, you need to examine the style and construction of the piece.

Wrought-iron pieces are typically made from strips or bars that are bent and forged into shape and riveted or welded together. Steel may be used in a similar way. Cast-iron pieces may be solid or hollow, depending on their size and shape; since they are made in a mould, moulding lines (seams formed where the parts of the mould were joined) are a good indication that an item is cast iron. Another indication of the use of cast iron is a granular surface texture.

Dealing with corrosion

Both iron and steel rust rapidly in damp conditions. In time, depending on the alloy of the metal, corrosion will produce deep pitting or cause particles to expand and flake off. Keep ironware in a dry atmosphere or ensure the surface is well protected, for example by microcrystalline wax.

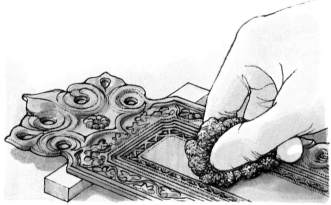

Light rust
To remove light rust, first treat the metal with paraffin for a couple of hours (either leave the piece to soak in the paraffin or brush it onto the surface). Rub off the rust with pads of fine wire wool, then wipe the surface and rinse with white spirit. Dry the metal and apply a paint finish, lacquer or microcrystalline wax.

Heavy rust
If a painted surface has failed, it is better to remove the old paint with paint remover before treating the rust. However, if it is important to preserve the paintwork, try to clean the rust patches only – the edges of the rust probably extend under the finish, so you will need to remove some of the surrounding paint. Scrape the rust with a scalpel. For large stripped areas, remove loose rust with a wire brush. Apply a commercial rust remover that includes an inhibitor, following the manufacturer's instructions. To leave a chemically inert surface, wash off the rust remover and dry the iron thoroughly. Protect it with two coats of metal primer and two of a compatible top-coat paint.

Sandblasting iron

Sandblasting is an efficient commercial process for removing old paint and rust that leaves the iron with a clean metallic surface. It is an abrasive process that is not suitable for most domestic ironwork, but it is useful for preparing old cast-iron fire grates. Finish the grate with black stove paint, black-lead wax or clear lacquer.

Protecting bright metal

Clean bright-metal parts with a spirit solvent such as white spirit or meths, followed, if appropriate, by a mildly abrasive chrome polish. However, steel is sometimes 'blued' (by means of a thin chemically produced coloured film) as a decorative finish and to inhibit rust – and an abrasive polish should never be used on a blued surface. Depending on the use, protect the cleaned surface with a clear lacquer or microcrystalline wax.

Repairing wrought iron and steel

Wrought iron and mild steel are malleable metals that are likely to bend rather than break. Straighten bent iron cold in a vice, using leverage or with the aid of a hammer. For thick sections, use a blowtorch to heat the metal first. Take great care if you have to use heat. If in doubt, place the work with a professional. Joints are usually riveted or welded; make simple rivet repairs using iron rivets (see page 42). Welding work can be done by a blacksmith or a local garage.

Repairing cast iron

Cast iron is a brittle material and may therefore fracture if struck hard or dropped. It is possible to have cast iron welded by a specialist, but for a break that is non-structural you can use an epoxy-adhesive. Ideally, repair the fracture immediately, in order to ensure that the joint is clean. If not, wash the broken edges with a solvent to remove grease and brush off any rust. Try the parts for fit, and then mix the two-part adhesive following the manufacturer's instructions. Apply it sparingly to the broken edges; press the parts together and hold them with clamps or with adhesive tape or a weight. When it has set, trim off exuded glue with a scalpel.

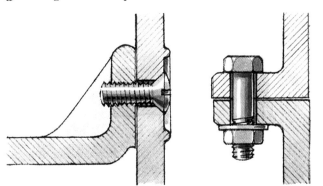

Repairing mechanical fixings

The individual parts of cast-iron products are sometimes held together with machine screws or nuts and bolts. Replace a missing screw with one that matches the thread cut in the metal, if need be shortening an overlength screw to fit. Hold the waste end in a vice and cut the screw with a hacksaw, then file the end smooth. Similarly, if the originals are rusted or missing, you can fit a new nut and bolt in a bolted joint, where the bolt passes through unthreaded holes in both parts.

IDENTIFYING THE MATERIAL

It is often difficult to identify gemstones and organic materials used in jewellery and other artefacts, as all natural materials vary slightly. And identification has been made even more difficult with the use of imitation and synthetic materials. A useful guide is to study the quality of the whole piece. If a piece of jewellery is finely made from precious metals, then it is likely to be of good quality and the gemstones authentic. Always have old jewellery assessed by a jeweller to establish its value.

Translucent gemstones are usually facet cut and polished to reveal their colour and brilliance, whereas semi-precious opaque stones are typically worked into a domed form known as a cabochon. Most of the semi-precious materials discussed here are organic in origin and, unlike precious gems, are relatively soft. They are also likely to display a variegated colouring, tend to be larger in size, and when used for jewellery are usually cabochon cut. Some, such as ivory, shell and jet, may have decorative tooling.

STORING SEMI-PRECIOUS MATERIALS

Treat and store semi-precious jewellery as you would fine-quality pieces. As the material is relatively soft, it is essential each piece is kept in such a way that it cannot be abraded by other, perhaps harder, jewels. Wrap necklaces in acid-free tissue paper. Keep brooches and rings in individual jewel boxes or in a shallow drawer or tray that has separate compartments.

Objets d'art made from these fragile materials should be handled with care. If displayed on open shelves, dust them occasionally with a soft cloth or brush to prevent a build-up of dirt. Ideally keep them in dust-free conditions in a glass-fronted display cabinet, which reduces the need to handle them for cleaning and the risk of accidental damage.

For further details, see under the individual materials.

SEMI-PRECIOUS MATERIALS

Humans seem to have an innate need to adorn themselves with decorative motifs and materials, as if to compensate for their plainness when compared with other creatures. This use of decoration is not restricted to personal adornment, but also takes the form of applied decoration for functional wares and artefacts.

It is perhaps not surprising that some of these materials are derived from animal as well as vegetable and mineral sources. Tortoiseshell, ivory, bone, sea shells, coral, pearl, amber and jet are just some of the so-called 'semi-precious' materials that are used for decorative purposes.

Although their intrinsic value is not as high as that of precious gemstones, they provide a wealth of beautiful materials that can be worked into a wonderful range of jewellery and other decorative items. Rare, unusual and finely crafted pieces are much sought after by collectors and command high prices.

It is worth sorting through trays of 'junk jewellery' and bric-a-brac in antique markets, as they often prove to be a source of neglected treasures, which you can restore or use in the repair of other pieces.

JET

Jet is a hard dense-black variety of lignite, which is a type of coal. It can be worked to a fine polished finish and was widely used for Victorian mourning jewellery. It was also used for carved decorative pieces made for display.

It is sometimes difficult to distinguish jet from black-glass imitations, but the real material is somewhat lighter in weight and has a warmer feel. Vulcanite – a kind of hard rubber, also known as ebonite – was also used to simulate jet. This can usually be identified by its colour, which fades to a rather dull brownish black. Jet is quite brittle and chips in a similar way to glass – though the chipped edges tend to have a matt appearance, unlike the shiny chipped surfaces of glass.

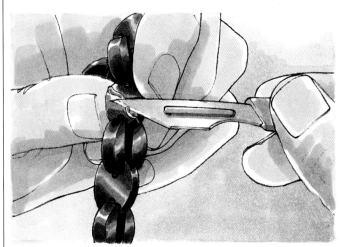

Making repairs

Jet is relatively brittle and may break if handled roughly. You can repair a clean break using a liquid cyanoacrylate adhesive applied sparingly to the broken edges. Test the parts for fit first, as this glue sets instantly. For breaks with ragged edges, use a two-part epoxy adhesive mixed with a black powdered pigment (available from suppliers of craft materials). This will also act as a filler. When the glue has set, but is not yet fully cured, use a scalpel to trim off any glue that has exuded from the joint. Once the glue has cured, polish the glue line where the adhesive is acting as a filler, using a mildly abrasive chrome polish. For small holes in a piece that is not subject to wear, you can use a hard black wax as a filler.

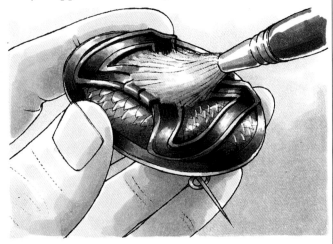

Cleaning jet jewellery

Brush off light dust and wash the jet with cotton buds, cotton-wool swabs or a soft brush moistened with a warm solution of washing-up liquid. Rinse with clean water in the same way and dry with a soft cloth. Do not use solvents such as white spirit, methylated spirit or acetone on jet, as these can harm it. You can brighten a dulled surface with a mildly abrasive chrome polish. Apply it sparingly, using a cotton bud to polish the surface. Wipe away all traces of the polish and wash as above.

RESTRINGING A PEARL NECKLACE

Check the thread of a necklace regularly. If it shows signs of wear, replace it before it breaks accidentally. Pearls are strung on silk thread that is available in a range of sizes and colours, so you should be able to match the original. Some types are supplied with a needle attached – but you can thread the end through the pearls, without using a needle, by stiffening the end with a quick-setting adhesive.

1 Arranging the pearls
Cut and remove the old thread, keeping the pearls in their correct order. If already loose, arrange them in order of size or colour, as required. To hold them in line, fold a length of card to make a V-shaped sorting tray.

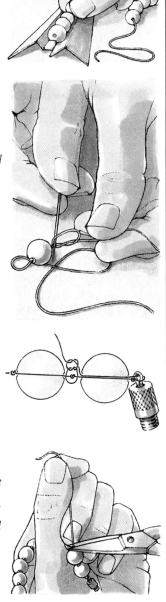

2 Knotting the thread
Make a half-hitch knot about 100mm (4in) from the end. Thread the first pearl up to it and make another knot against the bead. In this way every pearl is held individually, to avoid losing the whole string of beads should the thread break. The knots also prevent the pearls abrading one another. Use a needle to hold the loop of the knot against the bead as you tighten it. Fasten the remaining pearls in the same way. This method should be used for all good-quality bead necklaces.

3 Fitting the clasp
Tie off the last pearl, then pass the thread through the clasp ring and back through the pearl. Loop the end around the thread and secure it with a double-hitch knot.

4 Finishing the end
Pass the thread through the next pearl and then, while keeping the thread under tension, cut off the surplus flush with the second pearl. The end of the tensioned thread should pull back out of sight into the bead. Fit the other end of the clasp in the same way.

PEARLS

The iridescent white colour and natural bead shape of pearls have made them a favourite material for jewellery. They are drilled and strung on silk thread to make necklaces, or fitted to metal mounts to make rings, brooches and earrings. A natural pearl grows in an oyster over a long period of time and is formed by nacre (mother-of-pearl), which is composed mainly of calcium carbonate, building up on a small speck of grit. Natural pearls tend to be irregular in shape. Cultured pearls are produced by inserting a mother-of-pearl bead into an oyster and leaving it to form layers of nacre in the natural way; this forcing process is more likely to result in pearls of uniform shape. Man-made artificial pearls are moulded and coloured to look like the real thing, and can be quite convincing.

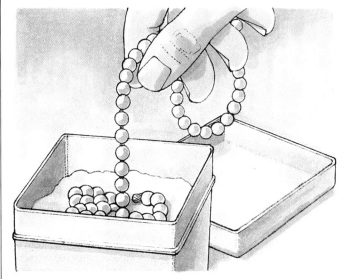

Cleaning pearls
The best way to keep pearls in good condition is to wear them. Pearls should not be cleaned with soap and water, as moisture can harm them. Clean them with a dry, light magnesium-carbonate powder available from pharmacists. Place the pearls in a sealable container, of suitable size, almost full of powder. Shake the container for a few minutes, then leave it to stand for about 24 hours. Remove the pearls and clean off the powder with a soft brush and cloth.

Alternatively, you can use a proprietary cleaning solution specially formulated for pearls. Following the manufacturer's instructions, dip the jewel into the pot, using the tray provided, and agitate it for not more than a minute. Lift out the pearls and wipe them dry with a soft cloth.

AMBER JEWELLERY

Amber is a natural resin exuded by ancient pine trees and fossilized to form a plastic-like material that ranges in colour from pale yellow to dark red. The beautiful colour of amber and its feel and ease of working have long been recognized. It has been used for applied decoration, jewellery and small artefacts since ancient times. Amber pieces sometimes contain seeds or insects trapped in the resin when it was fluid. Such inclusions add to their value for a collector.

Natural amber is readily polished and displays a variable translucent colouring. This has been successfully imitated in glass and modern synthetic plastics. Some imitations even include particles simulating those found in the natural resin. A simple test of authenticity is to heat amber by buffing with a wool cloth to detect whether it emits a pine-resin aroma. Natural amber also feels warmer than glass.

Ambroid is a reconstituted form of amber, chips of the natural material being heated and pressed together to form a larger piece. It is not as valuable as fine selected pieces.

Caring for amber

Amber is relatively soft and fragile, and artefacts made from it need careful handling. Keep fine-art pieces in a display cabinet and simply dust with a soft cloth occasionally. Store jewellery in a lined jewellery case, and wrap the pieces in acid-free tissue paper for long-term storage. Do not leave amber exposed to strong sunlight, nor in a position where it can be affected by hair sprays or perfume atomizers, as these substances can dull the polished surface irreparably.

Cleaning amber

Prolonged exposure to moisture or damp conditions can cause amber to lose its translucency and turn opaque. Although it is possible to clean very dirty amber with warm soapy water, it must be applied sparingly with cotton buds or swabs and rinsed and dried quickly. Buff the surface with a soft cotton cloth or chamois leather. The application of a little almond oil will help to restore the shine. Do not try to clean amber with alcohol or spirit solvents, as these can dissolve and matt the surface.

You can try polishing a matt surface, using a mildly abrasive chrome polish applied with a soft cotton cloth wrapped round your finger. Polish off with a clean soft cloth.

Making repairs

Although good-quality amber pieces should be repaired by a specialist, you can repair a simple break in lesser pieces yourself, using a clear cyanoacrylate adhesive. Apply a very thin film of the glue to the surfaces and press the parts together for an instant bond. Although not reversible, it will be less noticeable than an epoxy-resin adhesive, which would be visible through the translucent amber.

A clear all-purpose adhesive shares the advantage of being invisible, but the amber will be damaged if you have to use a solvent to reverse the bond.

REPAIRING BROOCH FASTENINGS

Brooches are often used for displaying large semi-precious stones, such as amber cabochons. They are usually fitted with simple metal mounts for pin-fastening to the garment. These fastenings often fail as a result of wear or rough handling.

Repairing a catch

Catches are easily crushed and often broken. Carefully re-form a simple bent catch, using a pair of fine-nose pliers. Take care not to overstrain the hook, as the weakened metal can easily break. If the catch is missing, fit a replacement made with a flat base, available from a jewellers' supplier.

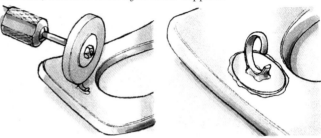

Grind off the remains of the broken catch, using a miniature power drill and abrasive wheel.

Bond the catch to the back of the mount, using a two-part epoxy-resin adhesive.

Straightening a bent pin

The design of the brooch pin will vary according to the quality of the piece. With most pin fastenings, the pin is sprung against a retaining hook. Some are fitted with a locking device to give greater security.

If the brooch pin is bent, so that it is slack in the catch, reshape it using pliers, working along the pin evenly.

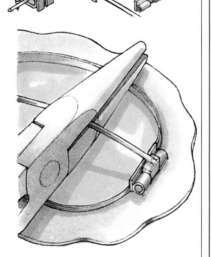

Increasing the tension

The spring tension of the pin is introduced at the hinge end by means of a stop formed in the hinge or pin. Adjust the stop or the pin using fine-nose pliers to provide sufficient spring in the mechanism to hold the pin in the catch.

Replace a broken pin with a new one, available from jewellers' suppliers, or have a jeweller make and fit one.

FITTING A SAFETY CHAIN

Fit a safety chain as a precaution against losing a valued piece of jewellery. Gold and silver chains are available from jewellers' suppliers. Brooch safety chains have a ring at one end for attaching to the brooch, and a safety pin at the other for fastening to the garment. Necklet chains have a ring at each end for attaching to the clasp; a bolt ring in the centre acts as a secondary clasp and allows the chain to be removed. Bracelet safety chains have a ring at each end for fastening to the clasp.

To attach a chain to the relevant item of jewellery, use fine-nose pliers to open the jump rings (see page 37).

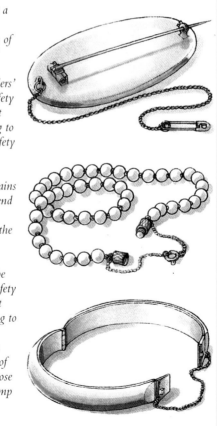

Ivory and Bone

Ivory is a hard, creamy-white organic material that is versatile as well as attractive. Elephant-tusk ivory is the most common type, but hippopotamus and walrus ivory also exist. Ivory is now a protected material, and most countries have imposed an import ban on it. It can be worked easily, and in the past was used for large and small figurative carvings, domestic wares, jewellery, and decorative veneers and inlays. Bone has similar properties to ivory and is used in much the same way, although solid pieces are generally smaller.

Ivory and bone can be differentiated by their weight and texture. Ivory is heavier than bone and has a dense, fine grain that polishes well. On close inspection, it is possible to detect concentric growth rings when it is cut transversely. Subtle coloured lines or bands formed by the layered rings may also be evident over the surface of the piece. Bone has a more porous texture, with dark flecks running along the surface of the polished material.

Old pieces of ivory mellow naturally to a warm yellow colour. Nevertheless, carved pieces were sometimes artificially coloured to accentuate the modelling. Old bone tends to be whiter in colour.

Although ivory was used as an applied decoration for other materials, ivory pieces were themselves sometimes decoratively engraved, painted, stained or gilded and were even inlaid with other precious and semi-precious materials.

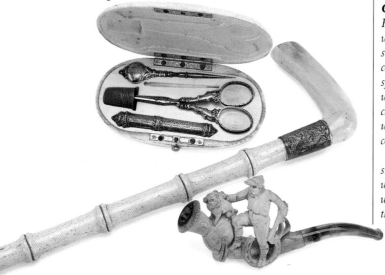

Caring for ivory and bone

Keep ivory and bone items in stable, moderate conditions, as changes in temperature or humidity can cause the material to expand or contract, causing distortion or splitting in a similar way to wood. Do not leave pieces close to a window, where direct sunlight, cold or damp conditions can adversely affect the material. Equally, keep it away from direct sources of heat, such as radiators or an open fire.

Cleaning

First remove any dust with a soft brush. Do not use a cloth on inlaid work, as you risk catching and damaging loose pieces. Wipe the surface of uncoloured ivory with a mild solution of warm water and conservator's liquid soap (1 part soap to 10 parts water), applied sparingly with cotton buds or cotton-wool swabs. Rinse with clean water applied in the same way. Dry the material quickly with a soft cloth to remove surplus moisture. Do not try to alter the colour by using bleach, as you will destroy its antique patina. Finish with a fine coating of microcrystalline wax to add lustre and protect the surface.

Inlays in wood can be dulled by accretions of old wax polish. If the size of the inlay allows, carefully clean off the old wax from it, using white spirit applied with cotton buds. Finish with microcrystalline wax. Where the inlay is too fine to clean with a solvent, just polish the whole surface with microcrystalline wax.

Caring for inlay

Ivory will shrink if subjected to overdry conditions, as will wood. Take care of inlaid furniture and decorative boxes, as the inlay can work loose and be easily damaged or lost.

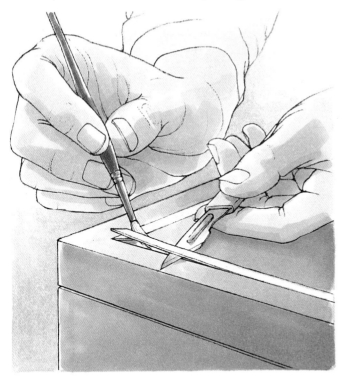

Regluing inlay
Reglue loose inlay with PVA adhesive. Work the glue under the inlay with a brush. Press the inlay into place and wipe all the surplus glue away carefully with a damp cloth. Cover the patch with a piece of polyethylene sheet and apply a weight to press the inlay flat. If the inlay has fallen out, carefully scrape out any old glue from the recess, then clean the back of the inlay and glue it into place.

REPAIRING CUTLERY

Ivory and bone were popular materials for cutlery handles around the turn of the century. Modern versions tend to use simulated handles made of plastic. Cutlery with ivory or bone handles should not be cleaned in a dishwasher, nor left to soak in hot water if hand washed. Exposure to hot water can cause the handles to distort or loosen.

1 Refitting a handle
The blade of a table knife has a tang that is glued into a hole in the handle, which can easily work loose. Pull the loose handle off and clean away any old glue from the tang and inside the handle. You may have to devise a wire tool to reach inside the handle, or use a suitably shaped needle file or a small gimlet or twist drill.

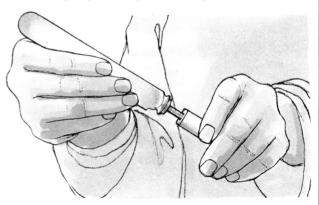

2 Fixing the handle
Check the fit and apply a two-part epoxy-resin adhesive to the tang and inside the handle. Do not overfill the handle, or hydraulic pressure will make it difficult to seat the blade. Push the tang into the handle up to the shoulder. Wipe off excess glue with methylated spirit, then leave to set.

TORTOISESHELL

Tortoiseshell is a translucent organic material that covers the surface of sea-turtle shells. The most common type comes from the hawksbill turtle. This plastic-like natural material is formed in polygonal plates that make up the domed shape of the shell. When heated, it softens and can be pressed flat or moulded into other shapes. Heat and pressure also enable it to be joined to create larger sheets.

Tortoiseshell has an attractive mottled colouring that is a mixture of yellow, brown, red and black. Its transparency also enables coloured backgrounds to be used to enhance the colouring. It has been widely used as a decorative veneer for furniture and boxes. The most extravagant examples were introduced by André Charles Boulle (1642-1732), who developed a marquetry technique featuring sheet brass and tortoiseshell cut together into ornate floral and geometric patterns. The method produced two sets of perfectly matched inlays, one the reverse of the other. The resulting panel was glued to the surface to produce spectacularly decorative pieces.

Tortoiseshell was also used in veneer or solid form for items such as small boxes, hand mirrors, combs, brush backs and buttons.

Recognizing the material

Genuine tortoiseshell is no longer available, so treat pieces made from it with care. Modern plastics are now used to reproduce the material and are commonly used for spectacle frames. Earlier examples of simulated tortoiseshell were made from celluloid or coloured horn. It is not always easy to distinguish the different materials. Study genuine articles in antique shops to get the 'feel' for real tortoiseshell.

Cleaning tortoiseshell

If items include inlay work, remove dust with a soft brush (not with a cloth), taking care to avoid catching the edge of raised or loose pieces. Clean the surface of tortoiseshell as you would ivory, using the minimum amount of warm soapy water. After drying, if it is lacklustre, treat it with almond oil to improve the colour. Apply the oil very sparingly and rub it in with a soft cotton cloth wrapped round your forefinger; repeat if the surface looks patchy, and wipe off any surplus. Alternatively, finish with a thin coating of microcrystalline wax.

If you are fortunate enough to own a fine piece of Boulle work, have it cleaned by a conservator.

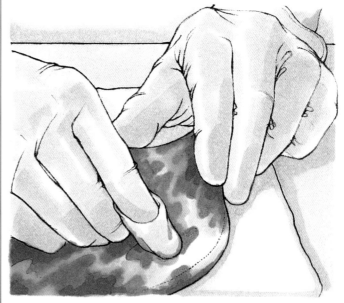

Reviving a dull surface
Abrasions or light fogging caused by overexposure to sunlight will leave the surface with a matt finish. Try rubbing them out, using a mildly abrasive chrome polish. Apply it with a soft cotton cloth wrapped round your finger, using a circular motion. Wipe off all traces of polish and buff with a soft cloth. Finish as described above.

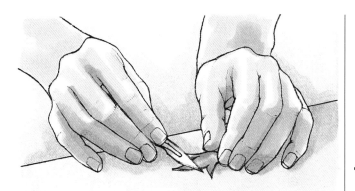

Making repairs

Loose pieces of inlaid tortoiseshell are not uncommon, as the animal glue used to fix them will weaken over time if subjected to moisture or fluctuations in temperature. If not already free, carefully remove loose pieces with a fine knife blade. Clean off old glue residues, then reglue (traditionalists prefer to use hot animal glue, but it is easier to use a modern PVA adhesive). Press the inlay into place, then clean off surplus glue, cover with polyethylene sheeting and clamp the inlaid surface flat or press it with weights.

For fractures in solid tortoiseshell pieces, such as a fretted hair slide or a buckle or button, glue the break with clear cyanoacrylate adhesive, applied sparingly.

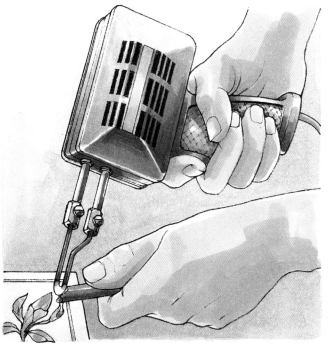

Missing inlay

Fill small spaces left by missing pieces of inlay with a coloured shellac stick used for furniture repairs. Choose a colour that has a similar tone to the tortoiseshell. Melt the shellac with an electric soldering iron to fill the recess. Allow the shellac to set, then carefully shave it flush with a sharp knife or chisel.

HORN

Horn possesses similar properties to tortoiseshell, and when cut into thin transparent sheets is used in much the same way. Like tortoiseshell, horn softens with heat and can be moulded into shape. In its natural form it was once used to make powder horns for charging muzzle-loading guns, and for domestic wares such as combs and handles for walking sticks and umbrellas. Most horn comes from cattle, but horn from other animals is also used. Deer antler, which is more like bone, is commonly used for cutlery handles. Maintain horn as described for tortoiseshell.

MOTHER-OF-PEARL

Mother-of-pearl is an iridescent calcium carbonate material, also known as nacre, that forms the inner layer of oyster shells and similar molluscs. Although it is a relatively hard and brittle material, it cuts well and is often converted into thin sheet that is used for inlay work, penknife handles, fan sticks and veneers. Mother-of-pearl can be carved, fretted and engraved; and is sometimes dyed to modify its colour. It is used for jewellery and decorative items, including dress and shirt buttons, and for domestics wares such as cutlery handles.

Repairing inlays

Like ivory and tortoiseshell inlay, mother-of-pearl pieces may loosen due to weakened adhesive or to movement in the base material caused by changes in humidity. Because the material is so brittle, do not try to reglue a raised piece that is still partly glued, as there is a risk of breaking it when it is pressed into place. When a piece has fallen out, scrape off old glue from the back of the inlay and the matching recess. Reglue the inlay with PVA or a clear all-purpose adhesive.

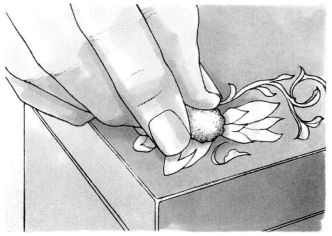

Cleaning mother-of-pearl

Like pearls, the shell material should not be washed with soap and water. For small objects you can use a pearl dip, available from jewellers. Use the dip solution to clean larger pieces or inlay, applying it sparingly with cotton buds or swabs. Rinse with cotton-wool swabs dampened with clean warm water, and pat dry with absorbent tissue.

If accretions of old wax polish have built up in engraved inlays, use cocktail sticks to scrape away most of the wax, then wipe away the residue with cotton buds dampened with white spirit. Take care not to contaminate the surrounding materials. Revive and protect the cleaned surface with microcrystalline wax.

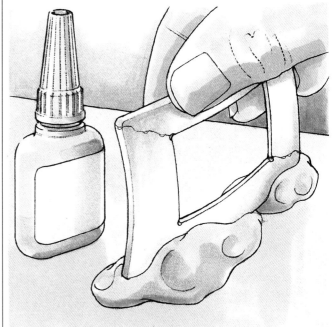

General repairs

Where items such as jewellery or hair slides have broken in two, glue them together with a cyanoacrylate adhesive if the break is small. If there is a larger gluing area that will not be subject to stress, then you can use a clear all-purpose adhesive. Refix cutlery handles as described for ivory and bone (see page 59).

CORAL JEWELLERY

Coral is a rock-like material composed of the calcareous skeletons of tiny marine animals. It forms into beautiful fan and branching shapes that provide the raw material for jewellery and small carvings. Although the most common type is probably red coral (which is a pinkish red), other colours are also found.

Coral is a hard, dense material that polishes to a fine finish. Thin pieces of branch coral are usually drilled and strung on thread to make necklaces and bracelets or made into brooches, using wire mounts. Other kinds of coral may be made into beads or cabochons for earrings and brooches.

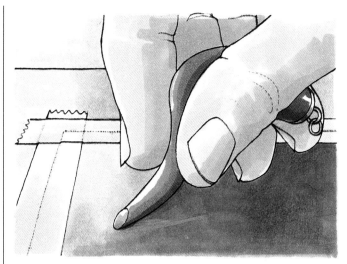

Reshaping coral

Red branch coral is often used for earring pendants, complimenting a necklace of similar design. Pendants tend to be made from larger pieces, and in the case of branch coral are usually handworked into irregular tapered shapes.

Should an irregular shaped pendant be slightly chipped at the tip, you can remove the blemish with abrasive paper, and the shape will help to disguise the repair. Tape a sheet of fine wet-and-dry paper to a flat board and lubricate it with water. Rub the coral across it to re-form the end into a pleasing shape. Apply mildly abrasive chrome polish and buff the reworked surface. If necessary, reshape the other pendant to match the reduced size.

Cleaning coral

Use cotton buds or swabs dampened with a mild solution of washing-up liquid or warm water and conservator's liquid soap (see page 58). Rinse with clean water, then quickly dry the coral with absorbent tissue or a soft cloth. Alternatively, use a proprietary pearl cleaner (see page 55).

Polishing coral

The surface of dull scratched coral can be polished with a mildly abrasive chrome polish, available from auto shops; apply it on a soft cloth or cotton bud, working with a circular motion. Alternatively, to revive the surface of fine pieces, use a miniature power drill fitted with a rubber polishing point coated with polishing compound. Wipe off all surplus polish and buff with a clean soft cloth.

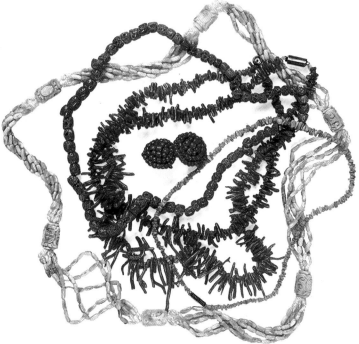

ORNAMENTAL STONES

Marble, onyx and alabaster are fine-grained stones that have a gem-like natural beauty when cut and polished. Marble, a metamorphic limestone rock, is probably the most common, offering a wide range of mottled and veined colours varying from white to black. It is used for statuary, vases, clock cases, bases for ornaments, table tops and architectural features such as floor and wall coverings. Onyx is a variety of microcrystalline quartz that has banded markings and is found in various colours, although green is the most popular. It is used for gemstones and for domestic wares, including decorative plinths for Art Deco figurines. Alabaster is an opaque or translucent variety of gypsum that is usually white in colour. Its fine texture has been exploited by sculptors for generations, especially in the making of ecclesiastical figurative carvings, but it is also used for domestic items such as clock cases or bases and vases.

These stones are relatively brittle and porous and mark easily, so handle objects made from them carefully. Fine or important works should be treated by professional restorers – but, with care, you can maintain most domestic items yourself.

Caring for ornamental stones

Moisture is the enemy of porous ornamental stones, causing natural salts, frost, mould and, more critically, acids from atmospheric pollution to attack the surface. If possible, they should therefore be kept indoors, in well-ventilated, damp-free conditions. Because they are porous, they also tend to absorb dirt and stains if not protected by a clear wax polish. Acidic substances, including drinks and foodstuffs, etch the polished surface. So quickly clean off any substances spilt on them.

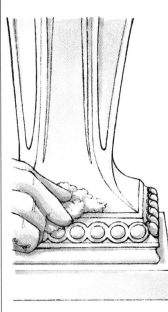

Cleaning marble and onyx

Of the two materials, marble is more likely to be encountered in the home, as it was once widely used for fire surrounds and table tops, urns and sculpture. The examples of treatment given here refer to marble, but are also applicable to onyx pieces.

Dust the surfaces regularly with a soft hog-hair paintbrush, taking care not to scratch the stone with the metal ferrule that holds the bristles. To be safe, cover the ferrule with adhesive masking tape.

If the surface has become lightly soiled or dowdy, wash it with a solution of conservator's liquid soap and warm water (see page 58), applied with dampened cotton-wool swabs. Clean a small area at a time – where applicable, working from the bottom to the top to avoid streaks. Rinse with swabs dampened with clean water. Pat dry with a soft, white cotton cloth.

Removing greasy marks

For heavy or greasy soiling, make up a solution of conservator's liquid soap and white spirit. Mix 1 part soap with 10 to 20 parts spirit. This is a powerful degreasant, so wear rubber gloves and protect your eyes against possible splashing. Apply the solution as described above.

Removing light water-soluble stains

If stains remain after cleaning white marble, try removing them by using a poultice made from shredded white absorbent tissue or an absorbent powder such as whiting. To lift water-soluble stains, mix the absorbent material with distilled water to form a stiff paste. Apply the poultice in a thick layer over the stain. Leave it in place so that the water can be drawn into the stone in order to activate the stain, which will be absorbed by the poultice as it dries. Wait until the poultice has almost dried, then remove it and rinse the surface of the marble with clean water before drying off.

Removing oily stains

Prepare a poultice (see opposite) using a solvent such as lighter fluid, acetone or clear alcohol instead of water. Apply a thick coating to the stain and cover it with a patch of polyethylene sheet, taped in place to prevent rapid evaporation of the solvent. For stubborn stains, you may need to repeat the process. Finally, wash the surface with a liquid-soap solution, as used on greasy marks (see opposite).

Bleaching white marble

For persistent unsightly stains in marble worktops or table tops, use 20-volume hydrogen peroxide. Brush this onto the stain and leave it to work, but monitor its progress; then wash the surface thoroughly. Wipe dry to get a better idea of the result. It may be necessary to repeat the process.

Repairing a chipped edge

Clean the surface thoroughly. Make up a filler of two-part epoxy-resin adhesive and white-marble or synthetic-onyx filler powder, as required. For coloured marble, add a small quantity of powdered pigment; you will need to experiment to get the right shade. Over-fill the depression and leave the repair to set. Either file the filler to the required contour or sand it with water-lubricated wet-and-dry paper; if need be, wrap the abrasive around shaped wooden blocks. Finish with very fine abrasive paper, then polish with microcrystalline wax.

Removing scratches

If an otherwise smooth surface is damaged by light abrasions, it is possible to remove them by hand – provided the remedy will not unduly spoil the piece. Rub out the blemish with very fine flour-grade wet-and-dry abrasive paper, lubricated with water. Where possible, work over the surrounding area to avoid creating a local depression. Wash away the slurry and polish the stone with white microcrystalline wax.

Mending broken parts

Make sure the broken pieces fit well and are clean. Prepare a two-part epoxy-resin adhesive and apply a thin film of it to both parts. Clamp them together, using rubber bands, adhesive tape or mechanical cramps as required. Ensure the joint is properly aligned. Leave excess glue to set, then trim it flush with a sharp knife. Wash the piece and finish with microcrystalline wax.

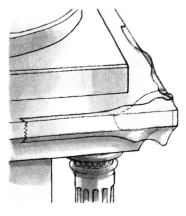

CARING FOR ALABASTER

Alabaster is softer than marble and onyx and can be easily scratched. It is also brittle, so needs careful handling. Exposure to water will cause the stone to dissolve, so keep it away from damp conditions and from plants that are regularly watered with a spray. Do not use water-based cleaning methods on alabaster. For general repairs, follow the methods described for marble.

Cleaning alabaster

Remove dust with a soft brush. To wash the stone, make up a spirit-based cleaner from concentrated liquid soap and white spirit. Mix 1 part soap to 20 parts white spirit. Apply the cleaner with cotton-wool swabs, working only a small area at a time. Rinse with white spirit, applied with clean swabs. Dry with a soft, white cotton cloth and then polish with microcrystalline wax.

A REASONABLE APPROACH TO RESTORATION

Given that china and pottery are inherently fragile, a great many old pieces are bound to exhibit some form of wear or damage, so don't feel you have to repair every chip or repaint slightly worn decoration. Although most collectors prefer pieces in perfect condition, a degree of damage is often acceptable – and it is certainly preferable to bodged or misguided restoration.

Before you decide on a course of action, ask yourself whether the particular piece will benefit from restoration. Most items look better after cleaning; it also makes sense to repair discoloured cracks and to remake badly fitting joints remaining from a previous attempt at restoration.

Items in several pieces are obvious candidates, but if you have no previous experience of regluing broken pottery or china, it is advisable to practise first on inexpensive modern crockery. Similarly, if your painting skills are not up to scratch, you can mend and fill the damaged piece but leave retouching till you have mastered the required techniques. The repaired item will look better with obvious but neat fillings than if disfigured by thick, inexpertly applied paint.

Always take valuable pieces to a professional restorer for repair, even if the damage or wear is slight.

CERAMICS

Antique china and pottery are much sought-after, both by collectors who acquire them for their aesthetic qualities, or for their rarity or financial value, and by people who simply enjoy using or possessing charming old pieces that cost little to buy yet have a great deal of life left in them.

Ceramics are relatively fragile and therefore prone to damage – indeed it is rare to find old china or pottery in perfect condition. Consequently, it is hardly surprising that a great many cracked, chipped and stained pieces are offered for sale at auction and in antique markets. With a little care and attention, you can restore these items to limited use or add an attractive piece to your collection. Admittedly, restored china does not command the same price as perfect pieces – but then neither do damaged ones.

CLEANING CERAMICS

Most collections, particularly those stored on open shelves, benefit from regular dusting and washing. However, the more china and pottery are handled, the greater the risk of damaging them – so when cleaning your collection, take your time and work methodically to avoid unnecessary accidents.

Carry only one piece at a time, having removed separate parts, such as lids, beforehand. Grip each piece firmly, if possible supporting it from below. It is not advisable to rely on the strength of handles or spouts. Never reach to the back of a display shelf to retrieve an item: remove the pieces in front first.

If you have a large collection of ceramics, clean only a small section at a time. This helps maintain concentration and avoids too many pieces piling up for washing and drying. Don't wear garments with long open sleeves when handling or cleaning ceramics – or heavy necklaces, which could swing against a piece of china.

Dusting your collection
It is generally safer to use a soft paintbrush or shaving brush to dust your collection – rather than a cloth or duster, which might become snagged on ornamental detail. Before washing ceramics, remove surface dust to prevent dirt getting washed into cracks and crazing.

Washing ceramics

Washing china merely to freshen its appearance does not involve prolonged soaking – nevertheless, you should be cautious about immersing repaired ceramics unless you know for certain that the materials used will not be harmed by water. Similarly, obtain expert advice before immersing very old or fragile items. Keep such items clean by dusting, and remove grubby patches with a ball of cotton wool moistened with warm water.

1 Washing by hand
Whatever its condition, never put old china in a dishwasher. Instead, fill a plastic bowl with warm water mixed with a little washing-up liquid. Wash your collection one piece at a time, using an artist's bristle brush to remove dirt from finely modelled figures or ornaments. Work slowly and deliberately.

2 Rinsing and drying
Rinse each piece individually in clean water, then lay it aside to dry on a tea towel or draining rack. Never stack one piece on another. You can dry some pieces with a clean cloth – but blot ornaments and figurines dry with thick paper towel, then if necessary finish the job with a hair dryer switched to a relatively cool setting.

Removing stains

Simply washing ceramics in warm water will not remove persistent stains. Dirt or grease that has penetrated into the body of the piece through cracks or fine crazing will need to be drawn out by soaking it in hand-hot water containing biological washing powder. The same treatment is required before attempting to assemble broken ceramics, to ensure that the edges of the shards are perfectly clean.

Superficial staining usually disappears after a relatively short period, but you may have to leave stubborn stains to soak for up to a couple of weeks, changing the hot washing-powder solution from time to time.

In all probability prolonged soaking will begin to break down old repairs (see page 70) – so, before soaking, examine each piece carefully for signs of retouching and glued joints.

1 Immersing in hot water
Fill a plastic bowl or bucket with a solution of washing powder in hot water. Immerse the stained item or broken pieces and leave them to soak for at least 20 minutes, swirling the water gently and scrubbing dirty cracks and broken edges with an old toothbrush.

2 Rinsing in clean water
As soon as you are satisfied with the result, rinse each item in clean cold water – fill the bowl to overflowing and leave the tap running for about 5 minutes.

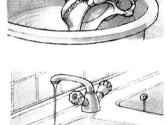

3 Drying the piece
Dry the pieces by hand with a soft cloth then put them in an oven, heated to 100°C, for about half an hour. At this point some items will exude still more grease from deep inside the ceramic body, in which case repeat the soaking and drying process.

Bleaching stains

For speed, many restorers resort to bleaching stained ceramics, rather than leaving them to soak. However, bleach can cause a stain to spread, particularly through absorbent pottery. Also, if you fail to rinse all the bleach out of the ceramic body, then it may eventually cause problems with overpainted repairs. However, provided retouching with paint or glaze is not required, bleaching is a viable option for cleaning hairline cracks in porcelain or stoneware prior to gluing. Seek professional advice before bleaching anything made earlier than the nineteenth century, and take great care with gilded pieces.

1 Preparing bleach
Wearing protective vinyl gloves, pour some 100-volume hydrogen peroxide into a saucer and dilute it with 3 parts water, then add a few drops of household ammonia. The fumes are not pleasant to breathe, so work in a well-ventilated area and wear a face mask.

2 Applying bleach
Soak the piece in clean water, then use tweezers to dip cotton-wool swabs in the bleach solution and apply them to the hairline crack.

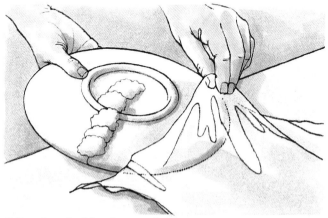

3 Leaving the bleach to work
Seal the piece in a plastic bag to keep the swabs moist. Keep an eye on progress for about 2 hours, then if necessary apply fresh swabs and reseal the bag. When the crack is clean, rinse the piece thoroughly in clean water.

DISMANTLING OLD REPAIRS

Restorers are often faced with the problem of having to dismantle previous restoration, either to replace old discoloured glue with a stronger modern adhesive or simply to improve on an unsatisfactory repair.

Soaking in hot water
In most cases you can break down old glue by leaving the piece to soak in hot water containing biological washing powder (see page 69) – which has the advantage of cleaning the item thoroughly at the same time.

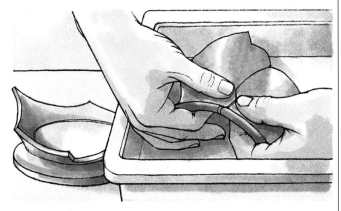

1 Easing the joints apart
After about 20 minutes, the hot water will begin to soften the majority of glues. Try easing the joints apart, but don't flex them or you may chip the fragile edges. Take care at this stage, because hot soapy water makes china slippery and it is all too easy to cut yourself on the sharp shards.

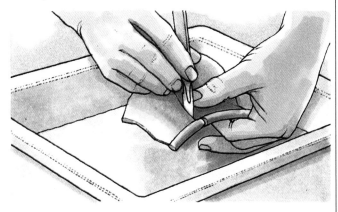

2 Using the point of a knife
Once a joint begins to separate, you can insert the point of a knife blade to prise the two pieces apart. Scrub the residue of glue from the edges with an old toothbrush, picking off any remaining specks of glue with the knife. Dry the shards in an oven (see page 69).

Using paint stripper
No amount of soaking will soften some modern glues, so that your only recourse is to apply a proprietary water-based paint stripper. Examine the piece beforehand to make sure there is no surface decoration that could be harmed by the stripper – and if necessary, apply stripper to the undecorated side of the piece only. Wear protective gloves and follow the manufacturer's recommendations.

Having attempted to resolve the problem by soaking in hot water, simply rinse the piece in cold water and apply the stripper. If you have allowed the item to dry, soak it again in clean water before proceeding.

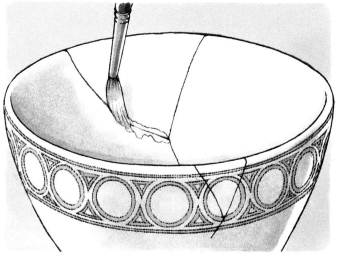

1 Applying paint stripper
Paint a gell-type, all-purpose stripper along each glued joint. Alternatively, dip balls of cotton wool in a liquid stripper and place them side by side along the joints. After 20 minutes, scrape the stripper from the surface and check for signs of movement. If need be, apply fresh stripper.

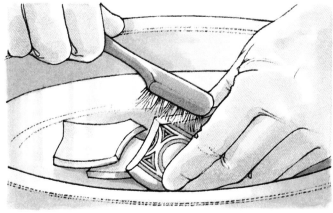

2 Washing off the stripper
Prise the joints apart, as described left, then transfer the pieces to a bowl of hot water and add some biological washing powder. Wearing eye protection in case of splashes, scrub and rinse the pieces thoroughly to remove softened glue and stripper (see page 69).

Removing rivets

Before the development of reliable adhesives, damaged pieces were sometimes stapled together with metal 'rivets'. Provided the joints are still sound, there is little point in removing rivets unless you find them particularly unsightly. However, if the piece requires additional restoration or is beginning to come apart, your best course of action is to remove the rivets and apply a modern epoxy-resin glue.

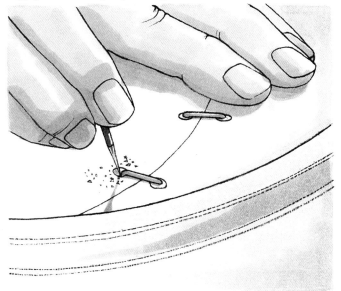

EXAMPLES OF EARLIER RESTORATION SHOW USE OF RIVETS AND DISCOLOURED GLUE LINES

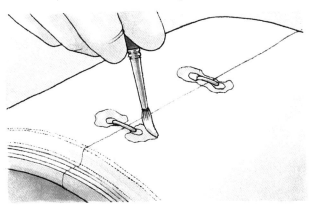

1 Picking the plaster out

The folded end of each rivet is located in a hole drilled in the ceramic body and embedded in plaster. Soften the plaster by soaking the piece in hand-hot water, then pick the plaster out with a pointed tool and pull out each rivet with pliers.

2 Removing stubborn rivets

Occasionally it proves impossible to remove a rivet until you cut it in half, using a miniature power tool fitted with a cutting disc.

Alternatively a rivet may be embedded in lead solder, in which case place the tip of a soldering iron on the rivet until the solder melts, then pull out the rivet immediately.

DEALING WITH RIVET STAINS

If subjected to damp or humid conditions, metal rivets can corrode and stain the ceramic body with oxides.

Neutralizing rust stains

To remove rust marks surrounding old rivets, use phosphoric acid sold in gel form for treating rusty car bodies. Wearing protective gloves, apply the gel to the stains and leave it in place for 15 to 20 minutes. Wipe the gel from the surface and, if necessary, make further applications until the stain has been reduced to an acceptable level. Finally, wash the area with water and dry it thoroughly with a hair dryer.

Swabs of cotton wool soaked in acetone or cellulose thinners may remove copper stains.

MENDING BROKEN CERAMICS

Every ceramics restorer must develop the ability to make accurate glued joints, for no amount of filling or repainting will disguise inept work. Edges to be joined must be scrupulously clean, as even the tiniest speck of dried glue can make it impossible to bring the surfaces snugly together.

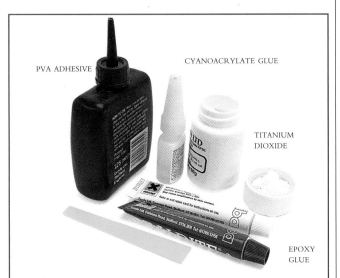

PVA ADHESIVE

CYANOACRYLATE GLUE

TITANIUM DIOXIDE

EPOXY GLUE

GLUES FOR CERAMIC RESTORATION

There are a number of adhesives recommended by professional restorers, but the most useful for amateurs is two-part epoxy glue, which can be bought from any hardware store or DIY centre. When the two components are mixed in equal proportions, the glue begins to set by chemical reaction, forming an extremely strong waterproof joint. Epoxy glue is practically transparent, but if there is the slightest risk of a perceptible glue line on white-bodied ceramics, add a pinch of titanium dioxide (a white powder available from craft-materials suppliers) to the mixed glue. Conventional epoxy glue sets hard within a few hours, but continues to gain in strength with time, especially if the repaired piece is warmed in an oven.

Epoxy glues are suitable for use with all types of ceramic, but some restorers prefer to use a water-based PVA woodworking adhesive to repair porous earthenware. In order to ensure a strong joint, the edge of each shard must be moistened with water before the glue is applied.

Should it be necessary, a PVA adhesive is reversible by immersion in water. Theoretically epoxy glues are irreversible, but in practice they can be softened with paint stripper (see page 70).

Cyanoacrylates (superglues) are marketed as general-purpose glues. Although they are rarely recommended by professionals for antique restoration, they do have their uses, especially for tacking together a complicated assembly (see opposite).

Repairing a crack

A hairline crack is worth gluing, not only to improve the appearance of a piece but also to prevent the crack extending further. Make sure the crack is clean by washing the item in a solution of biological washing powder (see page 69) or by bleaching it with hydrogen peroxide.

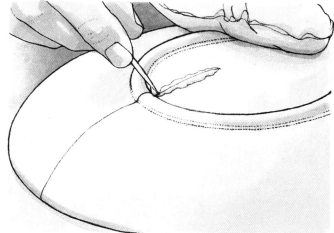

1 Introducing glue
Warm the damaged piece for 5 minutes in an oven heated to 100°C. Wearing oven gloves, transfer the piece to your workbench and use a cocktail stick to run epoxy glue sparingly along the crack. The heated ceramic will liquidize the glue and draw it into the crack. If the ceramic body is relatively thick, insert a razor blade to open the crack slightly before introducing the glue from both sides.

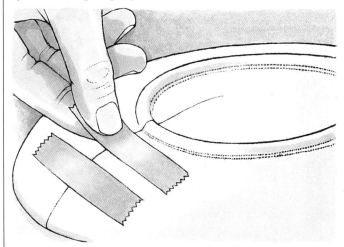

2 Strapping the crack
Remove the blade and wipe excess adhesive from the surface, using a cloth moistened with methylated spirit, then stretch one or two strips of adhesive tape across the crack. Put the piece back into the oven for 10 minutes to encourage the glue to cure. Let the piece cool, then remove the tape and pare the residue of adhesive from the surface with a sharp knife.

Assembling broken china and pottery

Gather together all the fragments of the broken item and wash them thoroughly, then dry them in an oven for 30 minutes (see page 69).

Before you mix the glue, make a 'dry run', taping the joints together to make sure you have all the pieces – and also, by rehearsing the procedure, to check that every fragment can be inserted without having to dismantle part of the assembly, and none of them is 'locked out'.

1 Begin with one of the larger fragments
Begin by sticking strips of adhesive tape on both sides of one of the larger fragments, so that the strips overhang the broken edge by half their length.

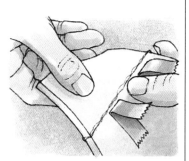

2 Applying adhesive
Use a cocktail stick to apply epoxy glue sparingly to the edge of the neighbouring fragment. Press both pieces together, rocking them slightly to exclude as much glue as possible and to encourage the edges to mate perfectly. Fold back each strip to prevent it getting in the way.

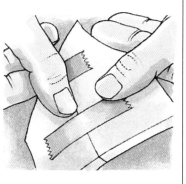

3 Strapping the joint
Holding the pieces together firmly, stretch each piece of tape across the joint. Wipe off excess adhesive and check the accuracy of the assembly by rubbing your thumbnail across the joint. If you can feel the slightest misalignment, slacken one or more strips of tape, adjust the fit and stretch the tape back in place.

4 Completing the assembly
Continue gluing one fragment to the next, following the sequence derived from your 'dry run'. When the assembly is complete, put it in the oven for 10 minutes. Once the ceramic is cool enough to touch, peel off the adhesive tape and pare off any dried glue adhering to the surface.

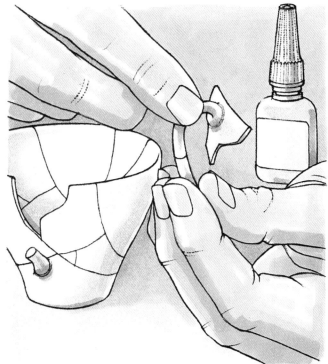

Tacking a complicated assembly

Strapping each joint with adhesive tape can be impossible when you have to assemble a great many small fragments. Instead, tack the fragments together, using tiny spots of cyanoacrylate glue, which sets in seconds. Work meticulously to ensure that each joint is perfect, dissolving the glue with acetone or cellulose thinners if you have to start again.

The completed assembly will be fragile, but strong enough to place in an oven, heated to 100°C, for about 5 minutes. As soon as you take the assembly out of the oven, run epoxy glue into each joint, as when repairing a hairline crack (see opposite). At this stage the job may well look very unsightly. Put the assembly back in the oven for 10 minutes, and the glue should then be hard enough for you to scrape the surface clean, once it is cool enough to touch.

DEALING WITH WARPED PIECES

When china or pottery breaks, tensions are released which sometimes cause one or more fragments to warp. This makes it impossible to align them in the conventional way.

One possible solution is to apply epoxy glue to both meeting edges, along half their length only. Strap the relevant section firmly with tape, then carefully pull the unglued edges together with more tape.

When the glue has set hard, remove the tape from the unglued section, introduce glue into the gap and tape the joint securely.

FILLING JOINTS

It is very rare for a ceramic piece to break cleanly. If you examine the fragments closely, you will invariably find that their edges are chipped and, in order to make a perfect repair, require filling after they have been glued.

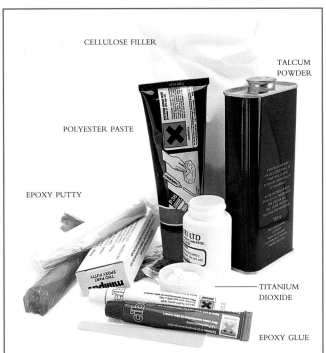

CELLULOSE FILLER

TALCUM POWDER

POLYESTER PASTE

EPOXY PUTTY

TITANIUM DIOXIDE

EPOXY GLUE

SUITABLE FILLERS

You can buy fine ready-made surface fillers and putties that are ideal for repairing ceramics, or make your own using epoxy glue as a base.

White two-part epoxy putty – which is available from many DIY outlets and modelling shops – begins to set as soon as the constituents are kneaded together. To make your own epoxy putty, mix titanium dioxide and talcum powder with two-part epoxy glue.

Polyester paste, manufactured for patching rusty car bodies, also serves as an excellent filler for ceramics: a red hardener mixed with the thick grey paste produces a pink filler, but you can modify the colour by adding a pinch of titanium dioxide.

These fillers can be used to repair a variety of ceramics, ranging from hard-paste porcelain to earthenware. For porous earthenware, however, many restorers prefer to use decorator's cellulose filler (either buy a tub of ready-made paste or mix a powdered filler with water).

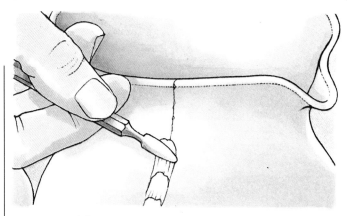

1 Inserting filler
Use a dental spatula or the tip of a knife blade to press filler into the minute holes and crevices, spreading it across each joint from different angles. Then run the blade or spatula along the joint to scrape the filler flush.

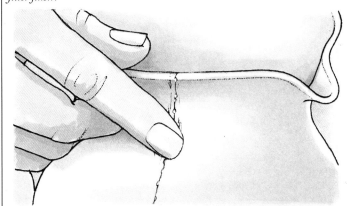

2 Removing excess filler
To smooth epoxy paste, moisten your finger tip and wipe it lightly along each joint – having to refill later is preferable to sanding down lumps of hardened filler.

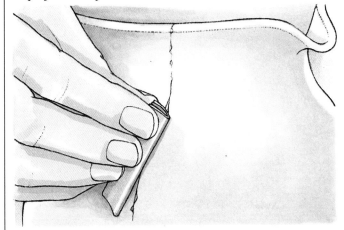

3 Sanding down
Allow the filler to harden thoroughly, then sand along all the joints with extra-fine (400 to 600 grade) wet-and-dry paper. To protect overglaze decoration from damage, restrict the sanding to as small an area as possible by cutting the paper into 50mm (2in) squares and folding them into narrow strips.

Repairing chipped edges

The vulnerable rims of earthenware and china often exhibit small 'shell' chips, especially decorative plates that have been hung from wire plate hangers. Fortunately this type of damage is easy to repair, using any of the putties or pastes recommended for filling glued joints.

Scrub chipped edges with hot water containing biological washing powder (see page 69). To help epoxy putty adhere, paint epoxy glue thinly onto the surface of the chip just before you fill it.

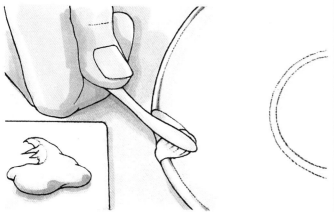

1 Applying filler
Press the filler in place, smoothing it into shape with a modelling tool or a moist fingertip.

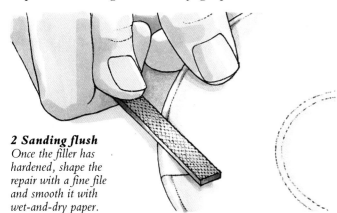

2 Sanding flush
Once the filler has hardened, shape the repair with a fine file and smooth it with wet-and-dry paper.

USING DENTAL WAX

As an alternative to modelling clay, you can use strips of dental wax (available from specialist craft suppliers) to make a simple press moulding (see top right). Smear petroleum jelly onto the area from which you intend to take the impression, then soften a strip of wax over a source of heat and press it into place. You may have to apply a second strip over the first to make the mould thick enough to retain its shape. Reposition the mould and fill it as described right.

Moulding a broken rim

If part of a rim has broken away, take an impression from an intact section of the rim and use it as a mould for reproducing the missing part. If the item is made with raised decoration, be sure to take the impression from the moulded side of the rim.

It is difficult to ensure a good bond to a very narrow broken edge. As a precaution, complete the filling but, before you sand it smooth, knock it out and glue it back in place with epoxy-resin glue, then fill the joint.

1 Taking the impression
Use a cotton-wool swab to moisten the area from which you intend to take an impression, then press a slab of children's modelling clay 12mm (½in) thick against the rim.

2 Repositioning the mould
Gently prise off the clay mould, taking care not to distort its shape, and locate it over the damaged section of the rim. To hold it in place, carefully fold the clay over the rim at each end of the mould.

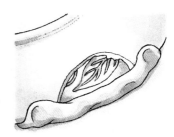

3 Filling the mould
Dust the clay mould with talcum powder to act as a release agent, and gently press epoxy putty or polyester paste into the mould. Take care to cover the inner face of the mould before building up the thickness of the damaged section — if need be, let the first layer harden before you attempt to fill flush.

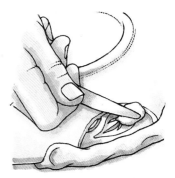

4 Smoothing the repair
Try to copy the contours of the piece as closely as possible, shaping the filler with a moistened filling knife. Leave the filler to harden overnight, then peel off the mould and smooth the repair with wet-and-dry paper. If one side of the repair includes raised decoration, you may have to remodel some of the fine detail, using epoxy putty.

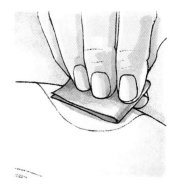

REPAINTING REPAIRED CERAMICS

Retouching damaged pattern and matching the background colour and glaze are the most difficult aspects of ceramic restoration. There are no shorts cuts: only practice and a good eye for colour will eventually produce successful results. However, it makes the work easier if you are able to buy the best-quality materials and equipment – especially if your budget will run to an airbrush that enables you to spray over filled repairs, leaving an indiscernible edge to the paintwork.

STOVE-ENAMELLING GLAZE

GLAZE THINNERS

ACRYLIC VARNISH

AIRBRUSH

SABLE BRUSHES

OIL PAINTS

ACRYLIC PAINT

Materials and equipment

You will need two or three artist's paintbrushes. Choose good-quality sable brushes that come to a fine point every time they are used.

An airbrush is a finely adjustable miniature spray gun operated by compressed air, which is supplied in aerosol cans or by means of an electrically powered compressor. Cans of compressed air are cheaper initially, but a compressor will eventually pay for itself if you specialize in ceramic restoration.

Use artist's acrylic paints to match the background colour of the piece you are working on, and a similar acrylic varnish to simulate the original glaze. Both the paints and the varnish are thinnable with water.

Alternatively, follow the example of professional restorers, who use a low-firing stove-enamelling glaze that is specially formulated for ceramics. This type of glaze sets after being heated in an ordinary domestic oven. Most professionals prefer an electric stove that maintains an accurate temperature, but you can use a gas oven or a solid-fuel range. To colour the background, add artist's oil paints to the clear stove-enamelling glaze and dilute it with cellulose thinners or the special thinner that is sold with the glaze. Don't be tempted to economize by buying cheap oil paints – they are likely to discolour after being heated in an oven.

If you are using an airbrush, it is imperative to work in a well-ventilated workshop equipped with an efficient extractor. You should also wear a respirator. Whatever equipment you use, illuminate your workbench with a simulated-daylight bulb to ensure accurate colour matching.

Painting by hand

Restoring paintwork and glaze by hand – using paintbrushes to apply the colour and transparent varnish – has the advantage of being relatively inexpensive and offers a measure of control that is appealing to novice restorers. However, the second of these advantages is somewhat illusory, as full control over any medium is rarely easy.

The techniques described here all involve using air-drying acrylic paints and varnishes – but it is also possible to apply stove-enamelling glaze by hand.

Matching the background colour

Mixing colours exactly is a process of trial and error guided by experience. Even a so-called white background is always biased towards the 'warm' or 'cool' end of the spectrum. Adding a speck of brown or yellow to white paint warms the colour slightly, while blues or greens cool it.

1 Mixing and testing the colour

In practice the best way to match the colour of the background is to use a white tile or saucer as a palette for mixing the paints, then brush a small spot of the mixed colour onto the body of the ceramic itself. Wipe it off immediately with a paper towel, and continue to adjust the colour balance until you are satisfied with the match.

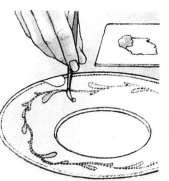

2 Applying the paint

Brush the paint smoothly onto the filled area, working from the centre of the repair towards the edges. You should avoid applying the paint too thickly, but it needs to flow out naturally and obliterate the filler without having to make a second application. Tentative brushstrokes tend to show as permanent marks in the paint as it dries.

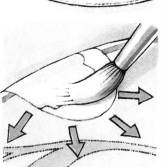

3 Feathering the edge

The aim is to cover the filled areas only, with the paint spreading as little as possible onto the undamaged surfaces of the ceramic. As you approach the perimeter of the repair, wash your brush and squeeze it dry, leaving the tip of the brush fan-shaped. Using very light strokes, drag the edge of the paintwork out onto the glazed surface until it is feathered out to nothing. Leave the paint to dry in a dust-free environment.

4 Rubbing down

If the new paint dries out to a slightly different colour or the surface is less than perfect, rub it down lightly with very fine self-lubricating silicon-carbide paper – a grey abrasive dusted with fine white powder available from DIY stores and modelling shops. After rubbing down, apply a second feathered coat of paint.

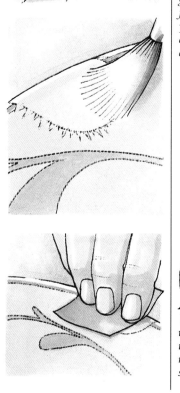

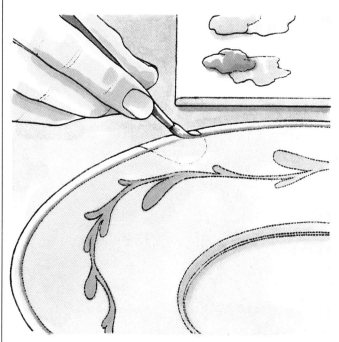

Recreating missing pattern

Once you are satisfied with your base colour, you can touch in any missing pattern or surface colouring. Use the remaining pattern as a guide to colour and shape, and apply the paint as described left, feathering off the edges of the new paintwork as much as possible. If you make a mistake or obliterate too much of the original paintwork, correct it immediately with the tip of a clean brush or a wooden cocktail stick moistened with water.

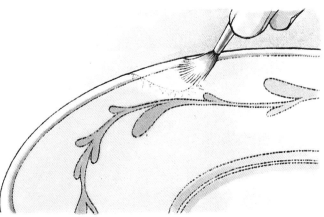

Applying clear varnish

When the coloured paintwork is dry, flow on a coat of clear acrylic varnish and feather the edges as you did the base colour. It is very important to protect the setting varnish from airborne dust – but if necessary you can leave it to harden, then rub it down and apply a second coat.

USING AN AIRBRUSH

A single-action airbrush has a button that releases the flow of air, while a separate control (usually mounted at the rear end of the handle) regulates the amount of paint or varnish delivered to the airbrush nozzle. This type of airbrush is relatively easy to use – having set the fluid control, you can concentrate on placing the paint exactly where you want it.

On a double-action airbrush, air supply and spray pattern are controlled by a single trigger. In the hands of an experienced artist the double-action airbrush is more versatile, but it is difficult to master initially. Whichever type of airbrush you decide to buy, check with your supplier that it is fitted with a fluid tip and needle capable of spraying relatively thick finishes.

Since the average restoration requires very little paint or varnish, an airbrush fitted with a small side cup or paint reservoir is convenient.

The various techniques described here use stove-enamelling glaze mixed with oil paints.

Controlling an airbrush
Hold the airbrush as if you were using a pen or pencil, in a relaxed grip with the first joint of your index finger resting on the control button. Drape the air hose over your wrist.

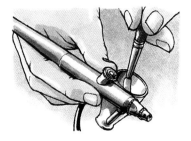

1 Mixing the paint
It is convenient to mix the glaze in the airbrush reservoir, then paint spots of colour onto the ceramic with a fine brush to see if you have achieved an accurate match (see page 77). Mix 50 per cent glaze and thinners, then gradually add the coloured oil paint as required.

2 Obliterating the filler
Because an airbrush applies very thin coats of glaze, begin by spraying the repaired areas with pure white glaze to highlight any blemishes that may require further filling and rubbing down.

Holding the tip of the airbrush close to the work, spray a narrow line of glaze along each filled joint. Take a clean paintbrush moistened with thinner and carefully wipe oversprayed glaze from areas of painted pattern.

3 Adding background colour
Put the sprayed piece in an oven, heated to 100°C, for about 45 minutes, then remove it from the oven and leave the ceramic to cool down. Spray over the repairs again, this time with glaze matched to the background colour. Return the piece to the oven for a further 45 minutes.

4 Adding pattern
Either use the airbrush to spray in areas of graduated colour or mix oil paint to the glaze and copy hard-edge patterns by hand, using a paintbrush. Heat the painted piece in the oven for another 45 minutes.

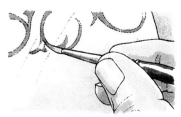

5 Spraying with clear glaze
Finally, spray over the restored paintwork with a coat of clear glaze. To simulate a matt glaze, add a pinch of fumed silica (a very fine white powder obtainable from pharmacists) to the stove-enamelling glaze. It is imperative to heat the final coat of glaze for a full hour.

SPECIAL EFFECTS

However skilful the repair, areas of freshly applied paintwork are sometimes a little too 'clean' to merge unobtrusively with old ceramic glazes and finishes. The solution may be to tint the final coat of clear glaze with the merest touch of oil paint to give it a suitably aged appearance. Occasionally it takes a little more to fool the eye.

Reproducing a crazed finish
The glaze on a great many old pieces of china and pottery is crazed, either deliberately during the manufacturing process or through shrinkage. Copy the pattern of cracks onto the body colour before you apply a coat of clear protective glaze. This requires a steady hand and either a very sharp coloured pencil or the finest brush and thinned paint or glaze.

Recreating unusual glazes
Metallic lustre glazes are notoriously difficult to replicate, and it is sometimes easier to settle for the effect of an old rubbed glaze rather than attempt a perfect finish. This is achieved by spraying the repair with the background colour of the original lustre glaze (say dark brown or grey) and then, when it is dry, overspraying it with a clear glaze containing a suitable blend of metallic powders (see right).

A similar technique is useful when you need to repair a dark-bodied ceramic finished with a translucent white glaze. First obliterate the filler with the dark colour, then apply a coat of thin white glaze that allows the background colour to show through.

REPAIRING GILDING

A great many antique pieces are decorated with gold paint or, in some cases, with real gold leaf. Gold leaf tends to be used only on old and valuable items, and it invariably pays to have these restored by an expert. Run-of-the-mill collectables can be retouched with gilt varnish, available from craft suppliers or by mail order. You can also buy gilt and bronze powders in various shades for mixing with turpentine or thinned stove-enamelling glaze.

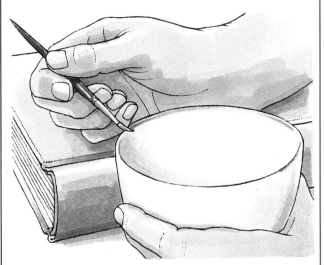

Gilding a rim
Antique bowls, cups and saucers are often finished with gilt rims that have to be retouched after a repair. Instead of trying to paint a straight line in the conventional manner, rest your painting arm on a support, such as a thick book, and revolve the piece against the tip of the brush.

USING AND DISPLAYING CHINA

Unless it is stored in extreme conditions, antique china does not suffer greatly from the effects of damp or dust. Airborne pollution can cause exposed paintwork to turn black, but this is easily remedied by rubbing it very gently with a plastic scouring pad and water.

The majority of repaired items are only suitable for the display cabinet. Heat or frequent washing is likely to discolour retouched repairs and may break down glued joints. Reglued handles are particularly vulnerable.

Even when old china is basically sound, check to see if the glaze is crazed – since fats from foodstuffs and sauces can penetrate and stain the ceramic body. Always wash and sterilize old ceramic items before using them for serving food, but don't be tempted to put them in a dishwasher.

Glass-fronted cabinets

The best way to display antique ceramics is probably in a glass-fronted cabinet. The pieces are kept relatively dust free, and they are safe from prying hands. Whether the cabinet is modern in style or a period piece to match the china is a matter of personal taste, but the latter can be bought very reasonably. Glass shelves are generally an advantage since they allow more light to be reflected into the cabinet; artificial lighting fitted within the cabinet itself is also an attractive option. Check that a cabinet is standing solidly – walking across a suspended wooden floor may be enough to start your collection rattling, with unfortunate consequences.

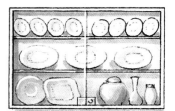

Veneered display cabinet in the Art Deco style

Open shelves

On open shelves, which may be the only realistic option for a sizable collection, china can be exhibited attractively and without distracting reflections in glass doors. However, you have to be prepared to dust on a regular basis. Choose or make shelves with a longitudinal groove to hold the rims of plates standing on edge. Alternatively, pin a narrow strip of wood to the shelf.

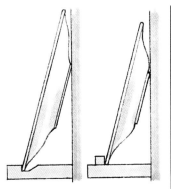

Plate stands and hangers

To display individual plates or cups and saucers, buy stands fashioned from plastic-covered metal rod or moulded plastic. Sprung-wire plate hangers are perfect for displaying china on a wall where you cannot install a cabinet or shelving. However, plate hangers can damage ceramics if carelessly applied. To prevent chipped rims, locate the wire hooks with care and slip thin card packing between the back of the plate and the hanger's coil springs to stop them rubbing the base.

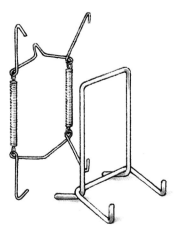

Old dressers are ideal for exhibiting ceramic collections

Display plates to utilize inaccessible wall space

81

A DURABLE MATERIAL

Although brittle, glass is a strong, durable material that is unaffected by atmospheric changes except for extreme conditions of moisture, light or heat. As a result, the glassware that has come down to us is often in excellent condition. If it has survived at all, it rarely needs much in the way of restoration.

Another reason for the scarcity of restored glassware is that there is only so much that can be done successfully to repair glass, even by experts. Other than craftsmen and craftswomen who restore stained glass and leaded lights, there are relatively few practising professionals who specialize in glass restoration. If you have very old and valuable pieces that are in need of care or repair, it is therefore probably best to seek out a ceramics restorer who is also experienced in mending glassware.

GLASS COLLECTABLES

Nowadays glass is such a commonplace and inexpensive material that we tend to take it for granted – but, because of its beauty and versatility, it has been used for thousands of years to fashion a staggering range of decorative and utilitarian objects.

Glass is made by fusing silica in the form of sand, flint or quartz with a flux such as potash, soda or lead at a high temperature. Adding various oxides to the mix produces coloured glass.

While it is molten, glass can be extruded, blown, moulded or rolled to create a seemingly endless variety of shapes. And when it has cooled, it is frequently embellished by cutting, etching, engraving, sandblasting, painting or gilding.

CLEANING GLASS

Except for fragile old glass that has been buried, perhaps for centuries, you can generally wash glassware in water without fear of harming it.

However, examine painted pieces to make sure the decoration is waterproof and not about to flake off; and don't immerse glass bottles and other containers that still have their original paper labels attached. Similarly, don't soak glassware that exhibits signs of previous restoration, in case the glue or paint that was used is not waterproof.

Wash antique glassware by hand – never in a dishwasher – and dust each piece before washing it, using a soft-bristle paintbrush.

1 Washing by hand
Fill a plastic bowl with hand-hot water containing biological washing powder. To avoid knocking glassware against the tap, place the bowl on a draining board or work surface, rather than in your kitchen sink.

Wash each piece individually, cleaning it with a piece of soft cloth, and use a paintbrush to tease the dirt out of engraving or finely cut decoration. When washing old glass bottles, you will probably need a specialized bottle brush to scrub the insides clean.

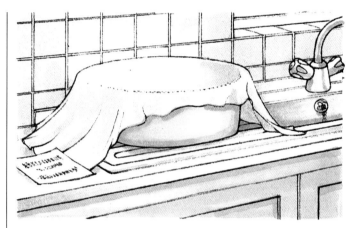

2 Soaking glassware
Leave very dirty pieces to soak for a couple of hours. Some glassware can be difficult to see in water, so lay a tea towel across the bowl and leave a note beside it to warn other people that there is glass soaking.

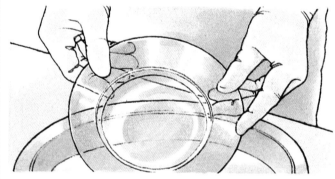

3 Rinsing in tepid water
Rinse in a bowl of clean tepid water. A few drops of methylated spirit added to the water will give the glass a pleasant sparkle.

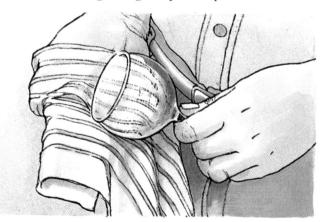

4 Drying glassware
Dry each piece carefully with a soft tea towel – don't polish drinking glasses with a twisting action, because you are liable to snap out pieces of glass. Instead, wipe straight from the bottom of the bowl towards the rim.

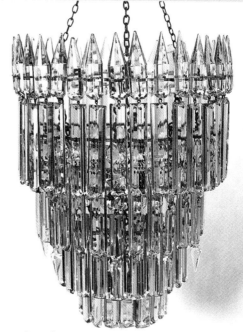

Drying decanters

It is important to ensure that moisture does not become trapped inside a stoppered decanter because it could turn the glass cloudy. Having dried the outside with a tea towel, leave the decanter upended in a plastic bucket to dry naturally. Dry the stopper separately.

Removing stains

As a rule, glass is affected by two types of staining – the white cloudiness associated with moisture and hard-water lime scale, and stains left by the contents (typically red wine).

To remove white water staining, try leaving the stain soaking overnight in denture cleaner, then rinse and dry the piece thoroughly.

Cover a red-wine stain with clear 'white' vinegar and leave it for 24 hours, then wash, rinse and dry the glassware.

If the glass has become etched, neither treatment will have the desired result.

Washing perfume bottles

Although many collectors keep antique perfume bottles purely for display, others like to use glamorous-looking bottles for their original purpose. Before you refill an old bottle, remove the smell of stale perfume by filling the bottle with methylated spirit and leaving it to soak for about an hour.

Keep refilling with fresh meths until the stale smell disappears, then wash out the bottle in warm soapy water and rinse thoroughly. Dry perfume bottles carefully – if need be, by drying the inside with a hair dryer at a cool setting.

Swabbing glassware

To wash glass that cannot be immersed in water, wipe the surface clean with swabs of cotton wool dipped in a warm solution of biological washing powder. Wash a large item from the bottom upwards, to avoid leaving dirty streaks on the glass. Swab the piece with cold water, then dry it with a clean tea towel. Finally, polish with methylated spirit on a cloth to make the glass sparkle.

Washing glass lustres

In the main, chandeliers are constructed from small glass droplets known as lustres that reflect the light in all directions. When they become covered with greasy deposits, nicotine or dust, lustres lose their sparkle and require washing. Although it is generally advisable to have a large chandelier cleaned by an expert, you may want to clean candlesticks or oil lamps hung with lustres yourself.

Assuming you are able to dismantle the piece, then you can wash individual lustres in a bowl of warm soapy water – but either remove the metal links before you immerse the lustres or make sure you dry the metal thoroughly to avoid rusting.

Alternatively, swab the lustres as described below left and polish them with a rag moistened with meths.

Cleaning enamel

Enamel is a form of coloured glass fused to a metal base. Among its many applications, enamel is used to make highly decorative jewellery, buttons and small boxes. Chipped or cracked enamel can allow moisture to penetrate, causing the metal backing to corrode and the enamel to flake off. Consequently, it is best to clean enamelled collectables by dusting with a soft paintbrush and to remove greasy deposits with cotton wool barely moistened with acetone.

REPAIRING GLASS

As a rule, once a piece of glassware is cracked or broken it can never be used safely for its original purpose. However, apart from the desire to preserve a piece of antique glassware, it is a good idea to stabilize cracked glass or glue a shard back in place as soon as possible to prevent an accident.

Don't attempt to restore valuable glass yourself; wrap it carefully and take it to a conservator.

SUITABLE ADHESIVES

Given that most glass is transparent, it is difficult to make an invisible glued repair. A restorer normally has to settle for a neat repair that allows the object to be displayed in a showcase, even though it will not stand up to close scrutiny. It is somewhat easier to make a discreet repair with opaque or dark-coloured glassware – but because it is difficult to fill repairs satisfactorily, you are still left with a glue line that is fairly obvious on close inspection.

Don't allow glue to spread onto the surface of etched or sandblasted glass, in case it dries as a shiny patch.

Take care when gluing together shards of glass – they are extremely sharp.

Ultra-violet-curing adhesive
Water-clear, glass-bonding adhesive is available from any good hardware store. When exposed to the ultra-violet rays present in natural daylight, the adhesive begins to cure rapidly, setting within 10 seconds in bright sunlight and after about 2 minutes on a cloudy day.

Since artificial tungsten light doesn't affect the adhesive, the most efficient method is to work under artificial light at a table in front of a curtained window; then once you have achieved an accurate glued joint, open the curtains to expose the adhesive to daylight.

Epoxy-resin adhesive
Ultra-violet-curing glue is not suitable for repairing opaque or dark-coloured glass. Instead, use a two-part epoxy-resin adhesive (see page 72). Before you mix the adhesive, warm the two tubes on a radiator to make the glue less viscous. Alternatively, it is possible to use a water-clear liquid epoxy adhesive, though it is not so readily available.

All-purpose adhesive
Although the repair will not be as strong as with the other recommended glues, you can stick broken glass with a clear all-purpose adhesive (this is not a cyanoacrylate glue).

Mending cracked glass
Cracked glass is only obvious because the air trapped inside the crack stands out as a silvery streak. If you can exclude the air, the crack is hardly noticeable.

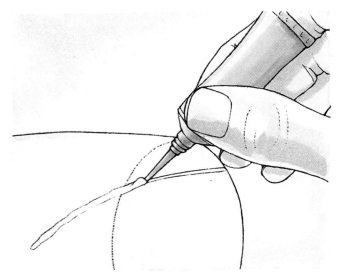

Run a narrow bead of ultra-violet-curing adhesive along a crack, then blow the glue into the crack to disperse the air. Wipe excess glue from the surface of the glass, using a cloth moistened with acetone.
Cure the adhesive by exposing it to daylight, then pare hardened glue off the surface by running a knife blade along the crack.

Reassembling broken glass
Before gluing a shard of glass back in place, clean the broken edges extremely carefully, using a cotton-wool bud dampened with acetone.

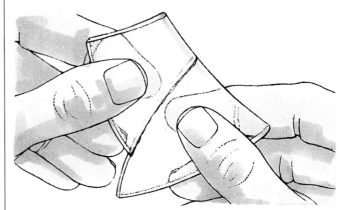

1 Applying adhesive
Check that there are no strands of cotton wool adhering to the glass, then apply ultra-violet-curing adhesive sparingly to one broken edge. Bring both pieces together, rocking them gently to exclude excess glue and to ensure the edges mate perfectly. Strap the repair with clear adhesive tape and, if necessary, exclude air from the joint as described for mending cracked glass (see above).

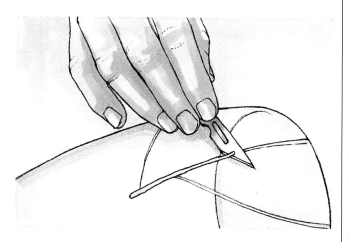

2 Cleaning up

Expose the glue to daylight. When the glue has set hard, pare any residue off the surface with a sharp knife and remove smears with acetone.

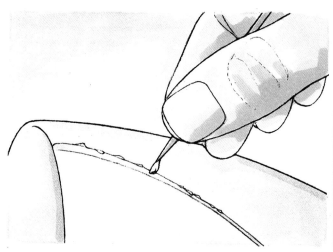

3 Filling small chips

As glass seldom breaks cleanly, you can usually detect small holes along the joint where tiny pieces of glass were chipped off the broken edges. Although it is impossible to make an invisible repair, you can improve on the appearance of a chipped joint by applying a tiny droplet of ultra-violet-curing glue to each hole.

Stretch transparent adhesive tape across the repair and rub it down. Leave the glue to cure, then carefully peel off the tape and pare the hardened glue flush with the surface of the glass. Burnish the repair with chrome polish.

Gluing a wine-glass stem

Gluing a broken wine-glass stem is not easy. Success or failure depends largely on the shape of the broken edges and whether they lock together without slipping sideways – a problem that is sometimes exacerbated when you introduce glue to the joint. Even when the repair is completely successful, don't be tempted to use the glass for drinking.

Supporting the repaired glass

With the glass standing on its rim, glue the repair in the usual way, using ultra-violet-curing adhesive. Support the base of the glass with strips of children's modelling clay while exposing the glue to daylight.

Removing glass stoppers

Although it is not exactly a repair, from time to time most glass collectors are confronted with the problem of having to remove a glass stopper stuck in a decanter or perfume bottle. This normally occurs when the piece has been stored with the stopper in place before the object is completely dry.

The solution is to apply a little olive oil. Apply the oil sparingly around the rim and leave it to seep between the stopper and the neck of the bottle or decanter. Then gingerly twist the stopper to release it.

RESTORING LEADED LIGHTS

Leaded lights are windows made from small pieces of textured or coloured glass held in place by a matrix of grooved lead strips known as cames. Spectacular examples were the glory of many a Victorian mansion, but by late-Victorian and Edwardian times leaded lights could be produced so cheaply that almost anyone could afford them. As a result, they are frequently found in quite small terraced houses, often in the form of colourful front-door panels or bathroom windows.

Any leaded light *in situ* is well worth preserving, particularly as a great many ornamental-glass windows were consigned to the scrap heap during the 1960s and 1970s. Some that were discarded survived and have found their way into the hands of antique dealers or, more often, architectural-salvage companies who can arrange to have them installed in your home.

Some collectors treat small leaded panels as works of art, and hang them in front of another window where they are displayed to advantage.

Supporting a panel
With the window frame laid flat on a bench, you need to support the horizontal glass-and-lead panel from below. Cut a sheet of plywood or MDF to fit the opening, and cover it with layers of newspaper to fill the gap.

Repairing leaded lights

It is quite surprising how much restoration work can be carried out to even badly damaged leaded lights. In the main this is skilful work, and any large-scale restoration that involves resoldering or replacing cames, as well as matching and cutting glass, should be left to an expert. There are professional restorers who will undertake the work for you, for very reasonable fees.

It is always worth getting expert advice before embarking on a course of action – but, provided the panel is accessible and not in a fragile condition, you might consider cleaning a leaded light and perhaps recementing the quarries (individual pieces of glass) to prevent them rattling.

Working on a bench

Even leaded lights in good condition are easily damaged unless you treat them with care. Pressing on the centre of a panel, for example, will distort the lead and cause the window to bulge – and if the lead is in poor condition, small pieces of glass may fall out. Consequently it is always advisable to remove a sliding-sash window or take a casement window off its hinges, so that you can lay it flat on a bench and work on both sides of the panel. You have little choice but to work on a fixed door panel *in situ*, but at least you can reach both sides – just take care not to put too much pressure on the leadwork.

Cleaning leaded lights

Because leaded lights are relatively laborious to keep clean, dirt tends to collect around the edges of the quarries (pieces of glass) and the leadwork becomes covered with white powdery deposits.

1 Cleaning the glass and lead

Unless the glass is etched or sandblasted, wash the lead cames with a soap-filled pad, then wipe them clean with a rag and wash the glass with warm soapy water. Wash a fixed window from the bottom upwards, to prevent dirty water streaking the glass.

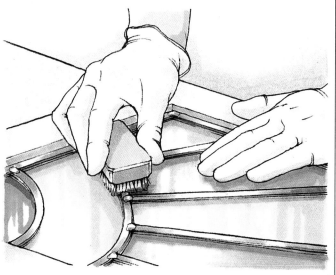

2 Colouring the lead

With a small amount of black-lead, fire-grate polish on a shoe brush, darken the colour of the lead by brushing across the cames (not along them). Provided the glass is clean, grate polish will not stick to it, even if the glass is painted. If the glass is not entirely clean, wipe off smears of grate polish with a rag moistened with white spirit.

Cementing loose quarries

The special cement used to hold glass quarries in the cames becomes brittle with age and tends to fall out. Restoring the cement consolidates a window panel and prevents loose quarries rattling.

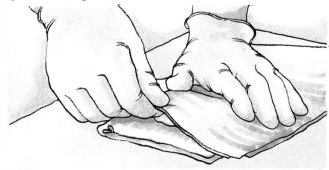

1 Preparing the cement

There is no need to buy special cement for a few loose quarries. Press some ordinary glazier's putty between sheets of newspaper to remove some of the oil, and knead it into a fairly stiff consistency. Mix in some black grate polish until the putty is a dark-grey colour.

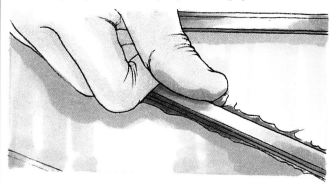

2 Filling the cames

Using your thumbs, press the putty under the edges of the cames that surround the loose quarries. Remember to fill both sides of the panel.

3 Removing excess putty

Sharpen a wooden spatula and use it to scrape excess polish from around the edges of the glass. Consolidate the putty by brushing across the cames with a shoe brush (see left).

USING AND DISPLAYING GLASS

So long as the glass is not chipped or cracked, there is no reason why you should not use antique glassware for the purpose for which it was intended. The greatest danger is the possibility of accidental damage, especially while cleaning glassware after use. Washing each piece carefully by hand (see page 84) lessens the risk considerably.

Long-term storage
Normal household conditions are perfectly safe for storing antique glass. The ideal storage cabinet has narrow shelves, so that you can see and retrieve every piece without having to reach over other items. Don't lift a glass by its rim – cup it in your hand and support the base from below.

When storing decanters, do not replace the stoppers. Cover the neck of the decanter with a paper towel, held in place with an elastic band, and store the stopper separately.

A glazed display cabinet is ideal for displaying antique glassware.

Displaying glassware in front of a source of light brings out the richness of coloured glass and incised decoration.

Displaying a collection of glass

In terms of protection, a glass-fronted display cabinet is probably the ideal place to display antique glassware; but unless the cabinet is lit sensitively, cut and engraved glass may not be shown to best advantage. For this reason alone, open shelving is favoured by some collectors – but never overcrowd the shelves, and don't risk hanging heavy pictures or mirrors above your glass collection.

Hanging mirrors

Wall-hung mirrors can be extremely heavy. Always replace the cord; or if the mirror is fitted with a chain, check its condition and make sure it is screwed securely to the back of the mirror.

Mirrored overmantels should stand on the mantel shelf and be screwed back to the wall above the fireplace. Metal mirror plates are usually screwed to the frame, close to its top edge. If the plates are missing, examine the back of the mirror for signs of fixings and try to buy suitable replacements.

Back lighting

Displaying glassware in front of a source of light brings out the richness of coloured glass and incised decoration. In a display case artificial lighting can be installed behind a translucent back panel, but natural daylight is a cheaper source of illumination.

You can stand glass on a deep window sill – provided that you do not have to reach across the sill to open the window, and there is no possibility of curtains blowing in the breeze. Narrow display shelves running across the front of a fixed light are another alternative; if possible, choose windows that do not receive direct sunlight.

Leaded-glass panels are obvious candidates for back lighting. Before displaying a panel, have it leaded around the edge by a specialist and ask the restorer to solder strong hooks to the lead so that you can suspend the panel from chains. When carrying leaded glass, hold the panel on edge with both hands; never carry it flat.

Displaying enamels

To provide protection against dust and airborne pollution, display small enamelled collectables behind glass – but not in direct sunlight or close to other sources of heat, since fluctuating temperatures can cause the metal backing to expand and contract, with the risk that the enamel may flake or craze. Don't store enamelled pieces in damp or humid conditions, in case the metal corrodes.

Secure an overmantel to the wall with mirror plates.

Nineteenth-century enamelled buttons in a glass-fronted display case.

THE CHARACTER OF WOOD

Patination is the result of various effects and treatments on the surface of the material over a period of time. To a collector it is a desirable feature, as the patina of age is not easy to reproduce and so represents a mark of authenticity. It is also aesthetically pleasing.

The patination of wood varies according to species. Some woods darken with age, others lighten. Ingrained dirt, surface damage, wear marks, and the absorption and accumulation of oil, wax or other finishes all contribute to the character of the material. It is therefore important to preserve the patina and, where possible, to keep cleaning and repair work to a superficial level.

With increased awareness of the need for conservation, many imported exotic woods are now listed as endangered species and are becoming more difficult to find. Rather than dispose of old non-repairable items of woodwork – particularly if they include exotic wood – store them as a valuable source of material for other repair projects. The colour of old wood also makes it more suitable than new unfinished wood for patch repairs.

WOODEN COLLECTABLES

We only have to glance at the wooden objects and artefacts around us to appreciate the variety of indigenous and exotic species used to produce all manner of functional and decorative handmade and machine-made wares. So versatile is wood as a workable material that it can be used to make items ranging from small simple artefacts, such as buttons, to magnificent marquetry-covered cabinets and even entire buildings. Indeed, so varied are the properties and appearance of wood that no two pieces, even from the same tree, are ever precisely the same.

In addition to furniture, the chances are that anyone interested in old things is likely to have bought, inherited or been given items of woodwork, such as clocks, tea caddies, jewellery boxes, gramophones, chess sets, carvings and wood-framed mirrors, or even old woodworking tools for display.

Provided pieces are well cared for, there is no reason why they should not continue to delight collectors for generations to come. You can undertake a number of maintenance tasks yourself – but seek the advice of a specialist restorer if you acquire an important or valuable piece in need of restoration or repair.

CLEANING WOOD

Over a period of time dirt, held by an accumulation of old wax or oil, can form a dull film over the surface, masking the rich colour and figure of the wood. With careful cleaning, the true colours of the material can be revealed without harming the natural aged patina. Do not overclean the surfaces or use harsh abrasives, as you risk wearing through the finish. Nor try to remove the darker shading from mouldings and carving, as this gives form and character to the decorative detail.

Regular cleaning
Dust particles are abrasive and need to be removed regularly, with light cleaning, as necessary. Use a soft-cloth duster or dusting mop to dust the surface of sound wood. But don't use a cloth when dusting woodwork that has loose or missing mouldings, inlay or veneer, as you may catch and damage the weakened parts: use a soft brush. Polish with wax occasionally.

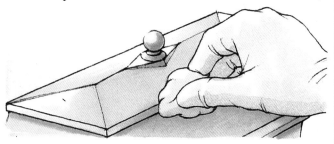

Removing grime
You can buy cleaners for removing dirty accretions of wax, or you can use white spirit. This is safe to use on all finishes and will not raise the grain nor harm veneer.
Apply the cleaner with a pad of cloth, working with the grain. Wipe off the residue with a clean cloth or paper towel dampened with white spirit and dry with a soft cloth. Finish with a light application of wax polish.

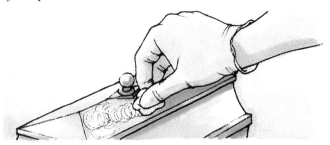

Reviving the finish
After cleaning, check the underlying French polish or varnish finish. If it looks dull, but is otherwise sound, you can revitalize it with a burnishing cream specifically made for polishing furniture or with any mildly abrasive cleaner, such as car-paint cleaner or metal polish. Apply the reviver with a soft cloth, and use firm pressure as you burnish the surface. Finish with a light protective coating of fine wax.

IDENTIFYING THE FINISH

In order to refurbish an old polished surface it is necessary to identify the type of finish. Traditional finishes for wood include oil, wax, French polish, cellulose lacquer and oil-based varnishes. Some modern varnishes are acrylic-based. The formulation of the finishes may vary, particularly ones of modern manufacture – although these are not likely to be encountered on antique pieces unless they have been refinished recently.

Wax, French polish, cellulose lacquer and acrylic varnish are reversible by dissolving them with the appropriate solvent. White spirit will dissolve wax. Methylated spirit and acetone will dissolve French polish. Acetone or cellulose thinners will also dissolve cellulose lacquer or acrylic varnish. Oil-based finishes are non-reversible, however, and are not affected by common solvents. These varnishes require the application of a chemical stripper to soften them.

To test which finish is used, apply each solvent in turn with a white cloth. Work on an inconspicuous part of the surface. The softened polish will leave a telltale mark on the cloth.

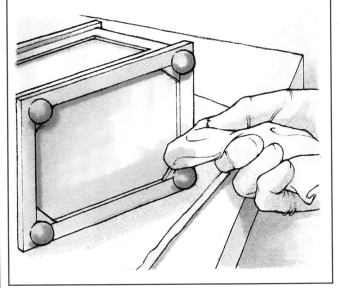

Caring for woodwork
To avoid the damaging effects of strong sunlight, change the position of wooden items placed near a window. Where possible, keep wood out of direct sunlight.

Keep items away from radiators, as central heating can cause wood to dry out excessively, leading to shrinkage problems. Use place mats and coasters to protect polished table tops – particularly those with French-polished surfaces – from hot crockery and spillage from drinking glasses. Wipe off spilt liquids without delay.

Attend to worn fittings, such as hinges or castors, before damage is caused to other components.

Inspect newly acquired pieces of old woodwork carefully for signs of furniture-beetle (woodworm) infestation, so you do not inadvertently introduce the problem to your home. Treat with an insecticide.

REMOVING SURFACE MARKS

Wood is a porous material that will absorb dirt and grease if not given a protective finish. However, traditional surface finishes can be marked by water, alcohol and other liquids, such as ink. Heat can also mark the finish.

Some marks will prove to be only superficial and are easily rubbed out; others may require the finish to be stripped and the wood refinished. Before undertaking remedial work, consider whether it is really necessary, as accumulated marks form part of the patina. However, if the marks are disfiguring, it may be better to remove them.

Dealing with scratches
Old scratches are an indication of wear and tear over the years, so may add to the character of a piece. However, you can rub out fine scratches that dull the polish, using a mildly abrasive cleaner applied with a soft cloth. Alternatively, disguise the scratches with a proprietary liquid retoucher. Apply it liberally over the scratched area and leave to dry for an hour or so, then remove the excess and polish with a soft cloth.

Removing white marks
White marks, often in the form of rings or round patches, are typically found in non-penetrating finishes such as French polish. The marks are usually only on the surface of the polish, and have been caused either by water or by a hot plate or cup being placed directly on the surface. Remove the resulting white bloom by rubbing gently with a mildly abrasive cleaner applied with a soft cloth. Take care not to rub through the finish, or you will need to rebuild it locally.

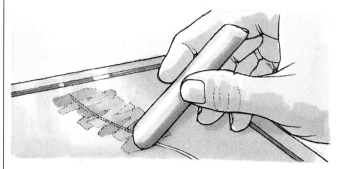

Using wax filler
Treat deeper scratches with a proprietary wood-coloured wax stick. These are made in a range of shades to blend with different woods. Rub the stick across the scratch to fill the recess. Wipe off the surplus and burnish the surface with a soft cloth. If necessary, finish with a wax polish.

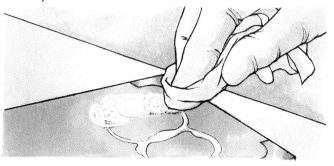

Removing etched marks
Spilt alcohol or cosmetic solvents can etch deep marks in the finish if left in contact with the polished surface. Try disguising the damage caused by these fluids by treating with a mildly abrasive cleaner. Alternatively, try reworking the finish with a pad dampened with the appropriate solvent, in order to even out the damaged surface.

If this proves to be insufficient, you will need to rebuild the finish. Carefully remove the polish with more solvent to form a patch with feathered edges, then leave to dry. Apply the appropriate polish to the patch with a brush and leave to harden. Rub down with very fine abrasive paper and finish with a burnishing cream.

Filling deep scratches
Fill deep scratches in French polish or varnish with a compatible finish. Use varnish straight from the tin, but pour a small amount of French polish into a small dish and allow it to thicken. Apply the finish liberally along the scratch, using a fine artist's paintbrush. Build up the finish, leaving it to set between applications, until it is above the surface level. Leave to harden fully, then carefully scrape off the surplus and finish flush with very fine abrasive paper followed by burnishing cream.

REPAIRING THE SURFACE

In the same way that scratches often add character to old wood, so too can other blemishes, such as dents, splits, scorch marks and wormholes.

A measure of their worth can be gauged by the fact that makers of reproduction furniture 'distress' new pieces with hot irons, chains and metal bars in order to produce an aged look. Before embarking on repairs, assess whether they are really desirable. Considerations of value apart, if damage disfigures an otherwise good surface, repairs are justified.

Repairing small holes and splits

Use coloured-wax sticks to repair wormholes and fine splits. These are made in a range of shades to approximate the colour of the most common woods.

Knead a piece of the wax between your fingers to soften it, then press it into the holes with a filling knife. Scrape off any excess filler once it has hardened, and burnish with the back of a piece of abrasive paper. Finish by applying wax or French polish.

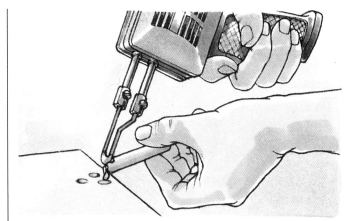

Using shellac sticks

Shellac sticks are a harder form of filler ideal for repairing larger holes. Use a soldering iron to melt the shellac into the hole. Overfill the hole and, while the shellac is still soft, press it home with a metal blade heated in warm water. When the filler has set, pare or scrape it flush with the surface and, if need be, sand with very fine abrasive paper.

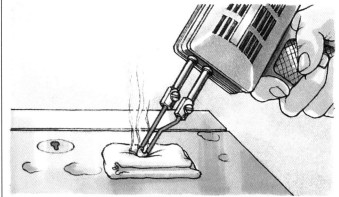

Raising dents

Impact from a hard object or pressure from a heavy weight can cause the cell structure of wood to be crushed. To remove the resulting depression, use a small artist's paintbrush to apply drops of hot water to the damaged area. The wood will gradually swell back to its original level as the water is absorbed. Repeat the process if necessary and, when the wood is fully dry, sand smooth the swollen fibres.

If the application of water is not sufficient, try steam. Place a damp cloth over the dent and heat it with a soldering iron. The steam should quickly cause the fibres to swell.

REMOVING DEEP SCRATCHES AND BURNS

Deep scratches across the grain or burn marks from
a cigarette are usually regarded as unacceptable. Depending
on the depth, it may be possible to erase the damage with
abrasive paper or by using a sharp cabinet scraper. In either
case you will be removing the surface of the wood and will
therefore need to use a wood dye to blend in the colour of
the exposed wood.

When using abrasives, start with the least coarse grade
necessary and work progressively through to the finer
grades. Always work along the grain, never across it, as fine
cross-grain scratches will be highlighted by the final finish.

Use a cabinet scraper for quicker results and more
control over a small area. Start by working the scraper
diagonally across the grain from opposite sides, then finish
following the grain. Although not always necessary after
scraping, you may need to sand the surface with a fine
abrasive paper to prepare it for finishing.

Filling holes and dents

Deep burn marks or woodworm or impact damage may mean
the wood has to be patch-repaired. The new wood will
require careful finishing to blend in with the original material.

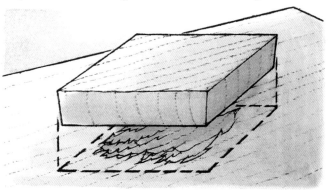

1 Cutting a surface patch

*The best way to make good a deep blemish in the surface of a panel
is to inlay a thick piece of matching wood selected for colour and
figure. Cut a diamond-shape patch that will cover the damaged area,
with the long axis following the grain. Plane a slight taper on each
edge of the patch.*

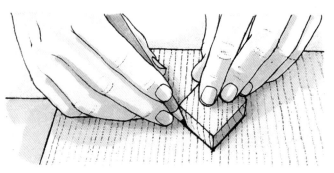

2 Cutting the recess

*Hold the patch over the damage and mark round it with a sharp
pencil. Carefully chisel out the waste, leaving a tapered recess that is
slightly shallower than the thickness of the patch.*

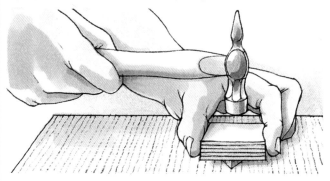

3 Fitting the patch

*Test the fit as you work. Once the patch is a close fit, apply PVA
glue in the recess and to the patch. Tap the patch into place, wipe off
excess glue and, when the glue has set, plane the surface flush. Sand
the surface ready for finishing.*

REPAIRING A BROKEN EDGE

If an integral moulding has broken off and is missing, you
have little choice but to graft on a new piece and shape it
in situ. First smooth off the broken edge using a block
plane, then prepare a patch of matching wood that is
slightly oversized and glue it into place. Use self-adhesive
tape to hold it in place if clamping is difficult.

When the glue has set, shape the contour with hand
planes, chisels and gouges, as required, then bring it to final
shape with abrasive paper. Where possible, make a shaped
sanding block to follow the contour.

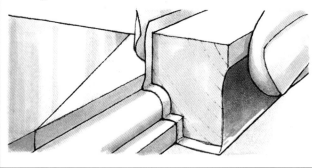

STRIPPING WOOD

Stripping the finish from old or collectable woodwork should be done only as a last resort, since much of the character and value will be lost. However, there are times – following fire damage, for example – when you have little choice. Small items polished with reversible finishes can be gently stripped with the appropriate solvent. Use white spirit to clean off wax, methylated spirit to remove French polish, and cellulose thinners for cellulose lacquers. Apply the solvent liberally with pads of very fine wire wool, working with the grain.

Using proprietary strippers

If you are faced with stripping a large area of wood, or when time is short, use a fast-acting commercial chemical stripper. You can buy a variety of types from DIY suppliers. General-purpose strippers – available in liquid, gel or paste form – are formulated to react with virtually all paint and wood finishes. Strippers for removing tough varnishes are also made. Most strippers contain harmful chemicals, so require careful handling – but this need not be a problem, provided that you follow the manufacturer's directions carefully. There are also 'safe' strippers that do not irritate the skin or give off strong fumes.

When it comes to washing off the chemical residues, you have a choice between strippers that use water or white spirit. Choose one that uses white spirit, as this will not raise the grain of the wood nor unduly affect the adhesion of veneers. Before using commercial strippers, contact your local authority to find out whether there are facilities for disposing of chemical waste.

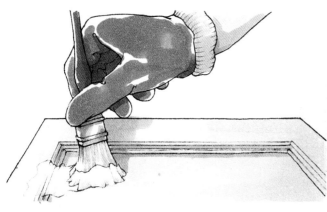

1 Applying chemical stripper
Read and follow the manufacturer's instructions carefully. Wear a face mask, goggles, protective gloves and, as it is messy work, old clothes. Pour some stripper into a jar or foil dish. Using an old paintbrush, liberally coat the surface with stripper. Leave it for up to 15 minutes to soften the finish, then test the penetration with a scraper. If the finish has not softened down to the wood, apply more stripper and stipple the blistered coating back into contact with the surface.

2 Removing the waste
When the finish is fully softened, use a paint scraper to remove the residue from flat surfaces. Work along the grain, not across it. Wipe the waste from the blade onto sheets of newspaper for safe disposal.

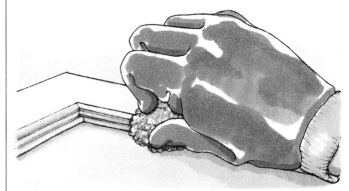

3 Dealing with shaped work
Use a sharpened stick to remove heavy waste deposits from mouldings and carved details. Follow this with balls of fine wire wool, turning them inside out as they become clogged – but use a nylon-fibre pad impregnated with abrasive particles when cleaning oak, as natural acids in the wood can react with trapped particles of wire, causing black stains. Use pads of wire wool (nylon-fibre pads for oak) to clean shaped parts turned on a lathe.

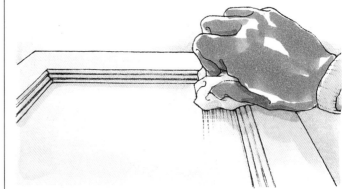

4 Cleaning the surface
Clean the remainder of the stripper from the surface and pores of the wood with pads dipped in fresh stripper, rubbing in the direction of the grain. Then wash off all traces of stripper with white spirit, applied with a cloth. Leave the wood to dry before preparing it for refinishing.

DEALING WITH WOODWORM

The discovery of furniture beetle (or woodworm, as it is commonly known) in old wood tends to alarm many people – to such an extent that they may consider destroying the piece to stop the infestation spreading. However, that is rarely necessary. Certainly infestation should not be ignored, but provided it is attended to promptly it can be contained and reinfestation prevented by simple methods.

Checking for woodworm
Flight holes about 2mm (1⁄16in) in size in the surface of the wood are likely to be the first signs of furniture-beetle infestation. However, it is the beetle's larvae that cause the real damage as they burrow through the wood.

The life cycle begins with the female beetle laying its eggs on rough unfinished surfaces, or in other convenient crevices. On hatching, the larvae proceed to burrow deep into the wood to feed, leaving behind them a maze of tunnels. After pupating just below the surface, they emerge as beetles, leaving the telltale holes.

Inspect all the surfaces of the wood for flight holes – paying particular attention to hidden parts, where activity may escape notice. Dark-coloured holes are likely to be the remains of an old, and now dormant, outbreak. Light-coloured holes could indicate a fresh attack. Check for signs of fine dust on the surface on which the piece is standing. This could be 'frass' (chewed-wood waste produced by the larvae), which would indicate recent activity.

Testing the wood
A large number of flight holes indicates a serious attack – but provided the wood is not weakened structurally, it can be saved.

Probe the infected area with a sharp pointed blade. If the wood offers no resistance or crumbles under pressure, it needs to be replaced. If the wood feels sound, it can be treated with a chemical insecticide.

Eradicating woodworm
You can buy woodworm-treatment fluid from most DIY suppliers – either in large cans for applying with a brush, or in aerosol sprays, or in an applicator for injecting into the flight holes. Follow the manufacturer's instructions when using these chemicals. Protect your eyes with goggles, particularly when using the injection method, and wear protective gloves.

Injecting the fluid
Insert the nozzle of the applicator into the flight holes and inject the fluid until it runs out. It is not necessary to treat every hole, as the chambers are usually interconnected. For this reason it is advisable not to lean over the workpiece while injecting the fluid, as it can spurt out from another hole. Wipe off excess fluid from finished surfaces.

Brush applications
Use a brush to treat large areas of unfinished wood. Pour fluid into a dish and coat the surfaces liberally. Allow it to soak in and repeat the application when the surface has dried.

Treat new wood in this way to prevent future infestation. You can apply any finish to the wood once it is dry. Also, as a preventative measure, you can maintain the finished surface with an insecticidal wax polish available from specialist suppliers.

BLEACHING WOOD

Persistent stains left in the fibres of wood after stripping the finish will require the use of bleach to remove them. Bleach can also be used to modify the natural colour of wood, should that be necessary when including new wood as part of a repair. You can make your own bleaching solution using oxalic-acid crystals or buy a proprietary two-part bleach.

Using oxalic-acid crystals

Oxalic acid is a traditional bleach for removing stains without altering the natural colour of the wood. It is also most effective for removing black iron stains caused by tannins in woods such as oak reacting with ironwork. You can buy it as crystals from pharmacists or restoration suppliers. Handle with care, as the crystals are toxic. Wear a mask, goggles and gloves while using oxalic acid – both in dry and liquid form – and ventilate the workshop. Prepare the solution in a glass jar or plastic pot (do not use a metal container) half-filled with warm water. Make a saturated solution by adding the crystals to the water, stirring gently, until no more will dissolve. Never pour water onto the crystals; always add them to the water.

Applying the bleach
Using a nylon or white-fibre brush, apply the bleach to the stained area and leave to form a crystalline film as it dries. If the stain persists, you may need to apply more bleach before leaving the wood to dry.
Rinse off and neutralize the bleach with washes of clean water. Wipe away the excess water and leave to dry. As the water will have raised the grain, lightly sand the surface smooth. Wear a face mask.

Lightening the colour

To change the natural colour of wood to a lighter tone (as well as for lifting stubborn stains), use a strong two-part bleach. The degree to which the colour changes will depend on the nature of the wood and the time allowed for the bleach to work. Where possible, make a test on a spare piece of similar wood or on an inconspicuous part of the work.

Using bleach
Following the manufacturer's instructions carefully, apply the first agent to the wood with a brush. Leave for about 5 to 10 minutes (the wood may turn a darker colour), then apply the second solution.
Allow the bleach to work. As soon as the wood reaches the required colour, stop the action by neutralizing the bleach with a wash of weak acetic acid made from 1 teaspoonful of white vinegar in 1 pint of water. Sand the surface of the wood once it is dry. Wear a face mask.

TYPES OF WOOD DYE

Wood dyes penetrate deep into the fibres of the wood and modify the natural colour, but they are not a finish in themselves. All penetrating dyes need to be protected with a surface finish. Some finishes, such as prestained varnishes, contain a colouring to achieve a similar appearance, but the colour largely remains in the surface film and is lost when the finish is removed.

Traditional penetrating dyes are supplied as powdered pigments for mixing with the appropriate solvent. This offers the widest choice for colour matching, but it takes experience to achieve the right mix. Ready-mixed dyes are easier to use and are available in a range of common wood shades.

Compatibility

You can mix practically any wood shade using compatible wood dyes or stains – as well as lightening the colour by adding more of the appropriate thinner. When choosing a stain, select one that will not be reactivated by the solvent in the finish you need to apply, causing the colour to bleed or become mobile as you work the surface.

Seal a solvent stain with shellac or sanding sealer before applying a varnish, lacquer or wax polish that is thinned with white spirit, turpentine or cellulose thinner. Use a spirit dye for any finish other than French polish. Water-based stains can be used with any finish, but test the results on an inconspicuous part first if you are planning to apply acrylic varnish.

COLOURING WOOD

Blending the colour of new work with the old is one of the most difficult tasks when repairing woodwork. It is made all the more difficult by the fact that any new finish, even if water clear, tends to darken the colouring.

To ensure a close match it is best to make up a colour-sample strip, using an offcut from the patch material. Various tests can be tried – by applying the appropriate finish only or wood dyes of differing strengths covered with the finish. Hold the sample strip against the work to judge the most suitable colour-and-tone combination. Err on the lighter side, as you can darken the colour slightly with a coloured-wax dressing.

Applying penetrating wood dyes
Set up an uncluttered work station, according to the size of the workpiece, in a well-ventilated, dust-free area. Wear PVC gloves and an apron, and old clothes if you are dyeing a large workpiece. You can apply wood dyes using a good-quality paintbrush, a decorator's mohair-pile paint pad or a wad of soft cloth. If you have a compressor or airbrush kit, you can spray them on.

Preparing the surface
Bring the surface to a fine sanded finish – making sure there are no cross-grain scratches or rough fibres, which would absorb more stain, resulting in a patchy finish. If need be, wet the surface with clean water to raise the grain then sand smooth when dry. This is essential before applying a water-based stain. Ensure that no glue remains on the surface, as this can affect the absorption of the stain.

Applying the stain
Pour enough stain to cover the repair into a shallow dish. Brush or swab the stain onto the wood in the direction of the grain, blending in the wet edges when working over a large area. Allow to soak in, then evenly wipe off surplus stain with a clean cloth pad.

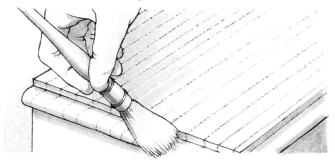

Staining end grain
The open cells of the end grain absorb more stain and will therefore appear darker than the other parts of the wood. To counteract this, partially seal the end grain with a brush coat of white shellac or sanding sealer. This will reduce the amount of colour taken up by the edge of the wood. Allow to dry fully before staining.

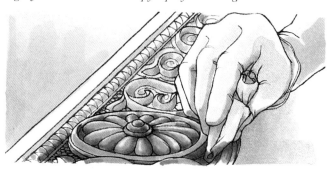

Staining carved wood
Apply the stain with a soft brush, working it well into the carved details while immediately absorbing surplus colouring from the hollows with a paper towel or cloth rag.

COLOURING VENEERS

Veneers bonded with water-soluble animal glue are best coloured with solvent or spirit-based stain. You can use any type of stain for veneers bonded with other glues. Apply the stain as you would for solid wood.

For a patch repair or a piece of marquetry, colour the veneer before gluing it in place. Dip the pieces into the stain to obtain an even colouring and leave to dry before cutting to size and shape.

REPLACING AND REPAIRING THE FINISH

Wood is normally treated with a finish to enhance its appearance and provide a protective coating. The finish also helps stabilize wood, as it renders it less able to take up moisture.

The type of finish will depend on the nature of the wood and how it is used. Most finishes are translucent, in order to allow the colour and figure of the wood to be enjoyed, but opaque paints are sometimes used to decorate and disguise poorer-quality woods.

Traditional translucent wood finishes include wax, oil finishes, oil-based varnish and shellac-based French polish.

Wax polish

Wax has a long history as a finish for wood. It can be used as a finish in itself or as a dressing to maintain the surface of other finishes, such as French polish and varnish. It is not a tough finish, but it is simple to apply and maintain – and over a period of years imparts a mellow quality that looks particularly attractive on old wood.

Types of wax polish
You can buy the raw materials for making traditional wax polishes from specialist suppliers, but it is more convenient to use one of the many ready-made, natural-wax products that are now available. Pale waxes in semi-liquid cream or non-liquid paste form give a beautiful mellow finish to light-coloured woods, while the darker-coloured 'antique' waxes produce a richer colouring for old sun-bleached woods and finishes. Microcrystalline waxes are fine clear waxes that do not stain even the lightest wood; they are used by conservators to protect and enhance a great many materials.

1 Applying a cream finish
Apply a brush coat of shellac or cellulose sealer to bare wood, and rub it down with fine silicon-carbide paper when it is dry. Pour the semi-liquid cream wax into a foil dish, and use a soft paintbrush to apply a liberal coating to the surface. Leave this coating to harden for about an hour.

2 Building up the polish
Apply a second coat with a soft cloth pad, working across the surface with an overlapping spiral action, then finish following the grain. Allow the wax to harden again, and repeat if necessary. Using a clean soft polishing cloth, vigorously buff the surface in the direction of the grain to bring up the shine.

1 Using paste wax
Prepare and seal the wood as for a cream wax. Load the face of a cloth pad with paste wax wiped from the tin. Work the cloth along the grain with a circular action, finishing with straight strokes.

2 Building up the polish
Use a ball of fine 0000-grade wire wool or a nylon-fibre pad impregnated with fine abrasive particles to apply another coat of wax about 20 minutes after the first. Work the pad along the grain only. Leave the wax to harden, and repeat to build up a protective coating. Finally, buff firmly with a soft cloth, or use a wax-polishing brush. A brush makes polishing carved work easier.

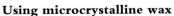

Using microcrystalline wax
Apply the wax sparingly with a soft cotton cloth. Use a brush for carved surfaces. Polish the surface with a clean cloth immediately after application.

Oil finishes

Oil finishes have long been used to preserve and enhance the beauty of wood. They are easily applied to any wood, producing a lustrous interior or exterior finish that needs little maintenance. Traditional linseed oil is still available for an authentic finish for old wood, but because it dries slowly it has now largely been superseded by faster-drying, hard-wearing modern alternatives. Gelled oil, a modern blend of natural oils and synthetic resin, has the consistency of soft wax polish. It can be applied to bare wood and, unlike other oil finishes, may be applied over existing lacquer and varnish finishes.

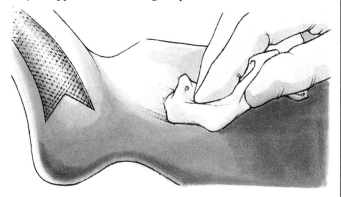

Oiling wood
Pour the oil into a foil dish and use a soft paintbrush to apply an even, liberal coat of the finish. Leave the oil to be absorbed before wiping the excess from the surface with a soft cloth. Allow to dry, then about 6 hours later apply a second coat and leave to dry overnight. Follow this with another coat, this time applied with a cloth pad. When it is dry, burnish with a soft cloth.

Oils that dry by oxidation give off heat as they dry, which can cause soiled cloths to ignite spontaneously. As a safety precaution, either soak oily cloths in water overnight or leave them unfolded to dry in the open air before you dispose of them.

Applying gelled oil
Apply gelled oil to bare wood with a cloth pad, rubbing it vigorously in the direction of the grain until it is touch dry. Apply two or more coats (depending on how hard-wearing it needs to be), allowing each application to dry for about 4 hours. Leave the finish to dry to a soft sheen. Over existing non-penetrative finishes, apply only a light coat of gelled oil.

Varnishing wood

Traditional oil varnish is a blend of natural resins, oil and solvent. Modern oil varnishes use synthetic materials. Oil varnishes – also known as solvent-based varnishes – dry by oxidation. As the solvent evaporates, the oxygen from the air is absorbed by the oil, causing a chemical change that prevents the dried finish from being reactivated by the solvent. Brushes must therefore be washed in solvent before the varnish dries.

The latest variants use acrylic resins and are water-based. These have certain advantages over oil-based finishes, as they are non-toxic and practically odourless. They dry quickly and are non-yellowing and non-flammable. After use, brushes can be washed out in water. Although acrylic varnishes are not a traditional finish for old woodwork, their properties make them worth considering for renewing a stripped surface.

Applying varnish
Varnish can be applied with a soft brush in the same way as paint; it is in fact virtually the same material but without the opaque pigments that are present in paints. Use a good-quality natural-bristle brush for oil varnishes, and a nylon-fibre brush for acrylic varnish.

Applying a sealer coat
For sealing bare wood, thin oil-based varnish by 10 per cent. Apply the varnish evenly with a brush. When the surface is dry, rub it down with fine wet-and-dry paper dipped in water; then wipe it clean, using a cloth dampened with white spirit.

Apply acrylic varnish full strength and rub down when dry. Do not use wire wool to rub down acrylic varnishes, as tiny slivers of metal can get trapped in the surface, causing black spots in the next coat. Wipe the surface with a cloth dampened with water.

Brushing the varnish
Brush on oil varnish following the grain of the wood, then work across it to spread the coating evenly. Working relatively quickly, brush towards the edge you have just finished, in order to blend the wet edges. Finally, 'lay off' along the grain with very light brushstrokes. Leave the varnish to set, then rub down before applying a second coat.

Apply acrylic varnish liberally across the grain and then lay off following the grain. When the surface is dry, after about 30 minutes, rub down and apply a second or third coat.

FRENCH POLISHING

Made from shellac dissolved in methylated spirit, French polish produces a high-gloss finish that enhances the colour and beauty of wood. It was particularly popular in Victorian times, when it was widely used for finishing close-grained woods such as mahogany, walnut and satinwood. Nevertheless, despite its look of quality, French polish is not a hard-wearing finish and is easily marked.

French polishing has always been regarded as a job for specialists, as producing the perfect finish requires skills that can only be developed with practice. However, the process only uses basic materials and it is possible for a patient and competent craftsperson to achieve a satisfactory result. To begin with it is essential that the wood is perfectly smooth, and the polish needs to be applied in thin layers over a period of days.

Preparing the work area

All polishing processes require a dust-free atmosphere – and none more so than French polishing. You also need to work in a dry, warm room. Where possible, work in front of a window or a well-illuminated area so the light falls across the surface of the workpiece.

You will need to make a rubber for applying the polish, and will need to have to hand some fine silicon-carbide abrasive paper, light lubricating oil, a soft brush and burnishing cream. If making a patch repair, choose the type of polish best suited to the colour of the wood or existing finish.

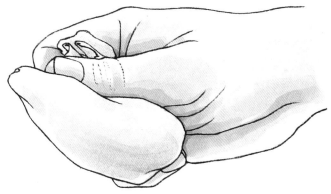

Making a rubber
The traditional method for applying French polish is to use a rubber made from cotton or fine linen cloth filled with cotton wadding.

Make the rubber a suitable size – so that it fits neatly in the palm of your hand – and roughly pointed in shape, so that you can work polish into corners.

Holding the wrapped pad in one hand, twist the gathered ends of the covering with the other, in order to compress the pad. Fold the twisted tail over onto the back of the pad to form a grip that fits into the hand and leaves a smooth sole to the pad.

Charging the rubber

Once you have mastered the art of wrapping the rubber, hold it in one hand unfolded. Pour some polish into the wadding, squeezing it gently until it is wet through but not saturated. Refold the covering and press the sole of the rubber against a clean flat surface to distribute the polish evenly and squeeze out the surplus. You will need to repeat this process as the polish is used up.

Storing a rubber

To keep the rubber clean and prevent it drying out, keep it in an airtight screw-top jar between applications. Stored this way the rubber will remain supple for months, and you will not need to discard it until the cloth is worn through.

Traditional wood finishers usually reuse the old wadding for applying French polish as a preparatory wood sealer.

BRUSHING SHELLAC

For jobs that do not warrant the laborious traditional French-polish treatment, time-saving brushing shellacs are available. These are specially formulated for brush application, being easy-flowing and slower drying in order to avoid brushmarks. The wood needs to be prepared the same way as for traditional French polishing.

1 Applying the polish
Load a soft brush with polish and apply it using straight even strokes, following the grain. Work relatively quickly, to avoid dragging the wet edge of the previous stroke. Use a light touch at the edges, as it is easy to wipe off too much shellac from the brush, causing runs. Brush out any runs as they occur.

Allow about an hour for the surface to dry, then rub it down with fine silicon-carbide paper. Apply one or two more coats in the same way.

2 Finishing with wax
A well-prepared surface should result in a bright gloss finish. If you want a more subtle glow, apply a wax polish with a pad of fine wire wool, working evenly along the grain. As brush-applied shellac builds to a good thickness, there is little risk of rubbing through – but do not overrub the surface, just in case. Buff the waxed surface with a soft cloth.

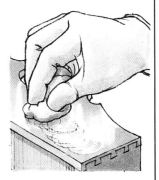

Applying French polish

French polish produces a high-gloss finish that highlights any flaws in the surface. It is therefore essential to prepare the wood thoroughly before polishing. The method explained here is for finishing a stripped flat surface.

Preparing the surface

Fill any surface damage (see pages 96–7) and sand the wood smooth; if required, apply a wood dye to colour the wood (see page 101). If you are treating new wood that has an open grain, you will need to fill the pores to create a smooth surface. This can be achieved by successive coats of French polish, which have to be rubbed down between applications, or by the less laborious application of a grain filler.

1 Applying a grain filler

Ready-mixed grain-filler pastes are available in a range of wood colours. Choose one that closely matches the colour of the wood. Make sure the surface is clean and free from dust, then apply the filler with a pad of coarse cloth. Work it into the grain using overlapping circular strokes.

When it is almost dry, rub across the grain with a clean pad of coarse cloth to remove the excess filler. Use a sharp stick to clean out filler from corners and mouldings. Leave to harden overnight, then sand lightly.

Filling stained wood

Applying filler over a ready-stained surface may result in some colour being removed when the surface is sanded; but if you fill first, there is a possibility the absorption will vary, resulting in an uneven colouring. To overcome the problem, apply the stain first then protect it with a brush coat of sanding sealer or transparent French polish – followed by the grain filler mixed with a little of the compatible wood dye.

1 Applying a sealer coat

Remove any dust from the surface of the wood, using a vacuum cleaner fitted with a brush attachment. Charge the rubber with thinned French polish and apply the first coat lightly, with long overlapping strokes following the grain, to seal the wood. As the work progresses, increase the pressure – to encourage the polish to flow. Cover the surface, keeping the rubber on the move, and do not go back over the work.

Leave the sealer coat to harden for about an hour, then rub it down with very fine silicon-carbide paper. Apply and rub down another coat if the first one is uneven.

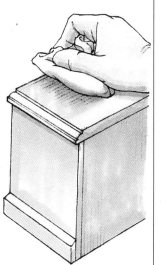

2 Bodying up the polish

'Bodying up' is the process of applying thin layers of shellac to build up the polish. Charge the rubber with full-strength polish; then, using a continuous movement and overlapping circular strokes, cover the entire surface with polish. Do not allow the rubber to rest on the surface, as it can stick and scar the polish. At the edges sweep the rubber off the work.

3 Using different strokes

To help build up an even coating, start again and apply some more polish – this time using a figure-of-eight movement. Follow this by using overlapping parallel strokes along the surface. Leave to dry for about 30 minutes, then repeat the whole process to build up three or four layers.

4 Lubricating the rubber

Depending on the size of the work, it may be necessary to recharge the rubber with polish as the work progresses. As the finish builds up, the rubber may begin to drag on the new surface. To overcome this, apply a touch of linseed oil on the sole to lubricate the pad, then continue as before. Use the oil sparingly.

After building up the finish, leave the polish to harden overnight. Repeat the process over a period of days, until you are satisfied with the condition of the surface.

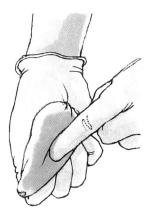

5 Removing the oil

At this stage the built-up surface is likely to display dull streaks. This is the residue of the lubricating oil. To remove it, add a little methylated spirit to an almost polish-free rubber and squeeze it nearly dry. Sweep the rubber across the work with straight parallel strokes, gradually increasing the pressure until the rubber begins to drag. Leave to dry for a few minutes; then repeat the process till the streaking disappears, leaving a high gloss. Leave to harden for about a week.

6 Burnishing the surface

If you are not satisfied with the final gloss, you can polish the hard surface with a special-purpose burnishing cream. Apply the cream with a soft cloth, rubbing vigorously, then polish to a deep shine with a clean soft cloth.

VENEERS

Veneer is a thin sheet of decorative wood bonded to a structural backing panel known as the groundwork. The groundwork of older pieces of veneered woodwork is generally made from solid pine or mahogany. Used properly, these woods provide a good base for veneer – but, like all solid woods, they are affected by atmospheric conditions, which often leads to a breakdown of the veneered surface. Today, stable man-made boards are used.

To identify veneered work from solid wood, look at the edges of panels to see if the grain of the wood is continuous. Also, check the underside or inside of the work to see if the wood is the same as the surface.

Although more susceptible to damage, veneer offers the use of exotic and unusual woods that would be impractical in solid form. Also, the figure of the wood can be varied according to the method used for cutting the veneer – giving an even greater choice of pattern, which craftsmen have successfully exploited for centuries.

Repairing veneered surfaces

Well-laid veneer should provide a trouble-free surface that can be maintained in much the same way as solid wood. However, it is less tolerant of moisture and changes in humidity.

Traditionally, veneer work was done using water-soluble animal glue and laid by hand with a veneer hammer or in a press. Animal glue is reversible with the application of heat and moisture and is preferred by professional restorers, although modern glues can be used for some repairs.

Most problems with veneered surfaces are caused by a breakdown of the glue, resulting in blisters or splintered edges. Poorly made or inadequately prepared groundwork can also lead to cross-grain fractures. In the latter case, it is usually necessary to remove, repair and relay the old veneer, or to replace it. The groundwork will also need attention. If you are in any doubt about your own craft abilities, take restoration work of this type to a professional.

Treating blisters

Blisters are particularly disfiguring on a polished surface, as they are highlighted by the gloss finish. Sometimes an area of loose veneer, caused by glue starvation, can be less obvious. To detect a patch that has become detached, tap the surface with your fingernails and listen for a hollow sound. As the treatment requires the application of water and heat, it will be necessary to remove the surface finish (see page 98).

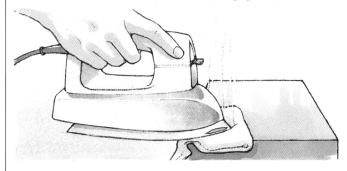

1 Flattening a blister
First try flattening the blister by reactivating the old glue. Place a damp cloth over the veneer and apply heat with an electric iron. The heat and moisture should soften the glue and also the veneer, making it more pliable.

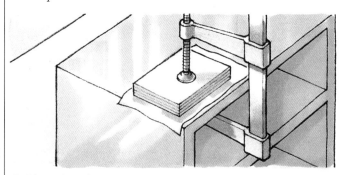

2 Clamping the repair
Press the veneer flat and then cover it with a piece of polyethylene plastic sheet and a flat block of wood. Apply pressure with a cramp or heavy weight until the glue has set.

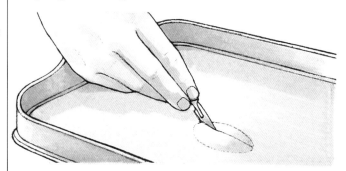

Adding glue
If insufficient glue was used in the first place, make a slit with a sharp knife along the blister, following the grain. Soften the veneer, as above, and work hot animal glue under the veneer with a brush. Press it flat and wipe away surplus glue with a damp cloth, then cover and press the repair flat.

Repairing damaged edges

The edges of veneered surfaces, cross-banded borders and edge lippings are susceptible to damage and frequently require repairs. Choose a veneer that closely matches the grain of the original wood. The colour can be modified, if need be, when the surface finish is applied (see page 101). The patch veneer needs to be slightly thicker than the surface veneer to allow for final sanding.

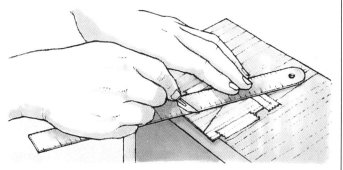

1 Patching the edge

Cut the selected patch veneer slightly larger than the damaged area. Take care to match up the grain as well as possible and tape it in place over the damaged portion. Using a scalpel and metal straightedge, make angled cuts through both veneers to form the patch and cutout.

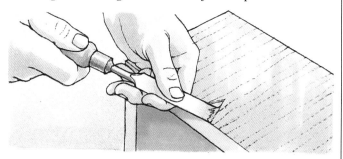

2 Preparing the cutout

Remove the patch and, using a sharp chisel, carefully trim away the remnants of the original splintered veneer from the groundwork. Dampening the waste can make it easier to remove. Scrape the surface smooth with a chisel held upright.

3 Gluing the patch

Apply hot animal glue or a modern cold-setting PVA woodworking adhesive to the patch and groundwork. Position the patch and hold it in place with gummed paper tape. Press it flat with a wooden block lined with polyethylene sheet and held in a cramp. When the glue has set, trim off the waste from the edge, holding the panel face down on a flat surface. Sand ready for finishing.

Repairing cross-banded borders

Cross-banding is used to create a decorative border around a veneered panel. A matching or contrasting veneer may be used, cut into strips with the grain running across the width of the banding.

Having 'short' grain, cross-banded borders are easily chipped. They can be patch-repaired – or if badly damaged, they can be replaced.

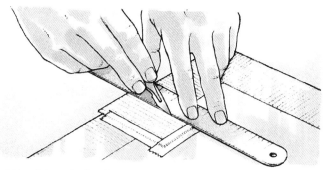

1 Patching the border

Tape an oversized piece of selected veneer over the damaged border. Make cuts square to the edge, through both veneers, on each side of the damage, using a scalpel and straightedge. Make a cut parallel to the edge between the two cuts, following the inner banding line.

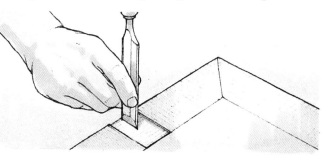

2 Fitting the patch

Remove the patch and, if need be, recut the lines in the border. Chisel out the waste from the cutout and scrape the groundwork smooth. Apply glue to the cutout and veneer. Tape the patch in place and clamp flat, using a block. When set, trim to size and sand the veneer.

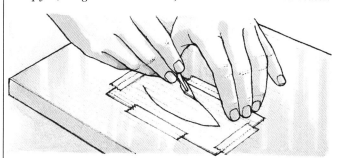

Patching the surface

Damage to the main surface of the veneer, such as a burn mark, can be patched in a similar way to an edge repair. Tape an oversized patch of the selected veneer over the damaged area. Take care to align the grain. Cut a 'boat-shaped' patch through both veneers. Trim the waste from the cutout and glue the patch in place. If the groundwork is also damaged, cut and fit a plug (see page 97) before patching.

INLAY AND MARQUETRY

Inlay is an intricate decorative technique whereby contrasting coloured woods – in the form of stringings, decorative veneer bandings or marquetry motifs – are set in recesses cut in a solid wood panel.

Stringings are single strips of solid wood made in a limited range of square and flat sections. They are used to outline decorative panels or borders and produced in 'white' and 'black' versions to contrast with the surrounding wood.

Decorative bandings are veneer-thick strips made in various widths and patterns from a variety of exotic and coloured woods.

Marquetry motifs are made from various natural and coloured veneers cut and assembled to form ornate floral and naturalistic designs. Parquetry, a form of marquetry, is made from veneers cut into geometric shapes. Marquetry and parquetry designs may be inlaid or made up and laid as a single sheet of veneer.

On antique items, you will often find that pieces of inlay have become loose, or are missing, due to the movement of the groundwork. Loose pieces can be reglued, but missing pieces will need to be remade. Ready-made decorative bandings and marquetry motifs in traditional designs are available from veneer suppliers.

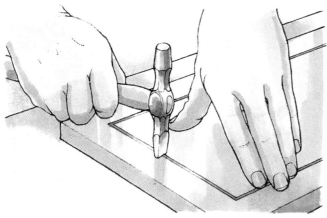

Fitting stringing
Clean the groove left by the missing stringing, using a narrow chisel or knife blade or a bradawl. Dry-fit the selected stringing into the groove and mark the required length. If the groove follows a curve, dampening the stringing will help it bend. Cut the stringing to length, apply animal glue into the groove, and press the stringing into place with a cross-peen hammer.

Repairing edge stringing
Clean the rebate left by the missing stringing with a sharp chisel held upright, or use a scratch stock. Apply glue and press the prepared stringing into place. Use short lengths of masking tape wrapped over the edge to hold the stringing while the glue sets.

Repairing decorative banding

Parts of the decorative elements that make up the banding may be missing. If they are insignificant, try filling the gap with a coloured-wax or shellac-stick filler. Where most of the banding is missing, you may be able to patch-repair the damaged strip, provided you can find a ready-made banding to match. If not, it may be necessary to replace the strip with one that closely resembles the original.

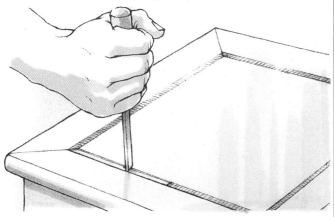

Replacing banding
Scrape the groove with a sharp chisel to remove dirt, old wax and glue. Trim the broken end of the original banding square, then chisel out the waste. Match the pattern and cut the new banding to length. Glue it into place and press it down with a cross-peen hammer.

PREPARING ANIMAL GLUE

Traditional animal glue is available in bead form from craft suppliers. It is prepared for use in a double or jacketed glue pot – or you can improvise by using a clean food-canister placed in a small saucepan.

    Quarter fill the glue pot with glue beads, cover them with hot water, and leave to soak. Place the glue pot in the saucepan and half fill the saucepan with water. Heat the water to soften the glue, making sure the glue does not boil. Stir regularly and add hot water as required, until the glue has a smooth, easy-flowing consistency.

Repairing marquetry and parquetry

Decorative marquetry and parquetry panels featuring complex designs in need of repair are best left to a professional restorer. However, simple motifs that may have one or two elements of the design missing can often be repaired at home.

1 Replacing a missing part
Clean out the recess left by the missing part. Tape a thin piece of paper over the design and use a soft pencil or wax crayon to make a rubbing of the recess. Using a water-soluble gum, stick the paper pattern to the selected veneer, making sure the grain is in the right direction. Leave to dry under a weighted block.

2 Fitting the veneer
Cut the part to shape with a scalpel, following the pattern. Use a metal straightedge as a guide for straight cuts; cut curves freehand. Check for fit and make fine adjustments by sanding the edges. Glue into place, and either press with a hammer or clamp with a block until set. Sand the patch lightly ready for finishing.

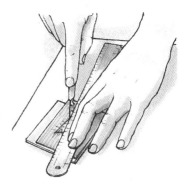

Shading veneer
Some traditional decorative motifs have parts of the assembly shaded to give a three-dimensional effect. If need be, you can reproduce a similar piece using heated sand.

Using hot sand
Fill a flat tin or foil dish with fine silver sand. Heat the sand on a cooker hob at a low setting. Cut the veneer a little oversize and insert the appropriate edge into the hot sand. After a few seconds, lift the veneer with tweezers to check the colour. Repeat as required.
    To test the final colour, as it will appear when finished, lightly sand the surface and dampen it. If satisfactory, cut and fit the part as above, making sure the shaded portion is correctly oriented.

THE FRAILTY OF OLD TEXTILES

Textiles composed of organic fibres begin to deteriorate from the moment the cloth comes off the loom. Expert conservation can retard the process, but nothing can stop it. For this and other reasons, textiles are more vulnerable than most antiques.

Exposure to strong light causes irreversible deterioration of the fabric, resulting in faded colours and brittle fibres. Damp conditions or high levels of humidity are also very damaging, leading to mould growth and in extreme cases causing colours to run. Dry heat can be harmful, too, as it causes the fibres to become brittle. Textiles need to be protected from airborne pollution and dust, which can stain and abrade fabrics and tarnish metallic threads. Dust also attracts harmful insects to textiles, which offer a ready supply of food for their larvae.

It can be difficult, if not impossible, to restore textiles once they have been subjected to a harmful environment. It is therefore essential to store and display them carefully, in order to protect your collection from some of the more obvious risks. Textiles also suffer from careless handling – so, when you are cleaning and repairing them, remove rings or other jewellery that might become snagged in the fabric and, to avoid the possibility of staining and cigarette burns, don't drink or smoke. Even the acidic oil we all carry on our fingers is harmful to antique textiles, so it is advisable to wash your hands before handling them.

TEXTILES

Even if you do not specifically collect antique textiles, you probably own and use an old tablecloth, or perhaps a fireside rug or some embroidered cushion covers passed down to you from your grandparents or a great-aunt. Textiles are common heirlooms – possibly because they seem never to outlive their usefulness, despite the fact that fashions change and you may no longer wear clothes you bought just a few years ago. Nevertheless, costume and accessories such as hats, bags and shoes are highly collectable. So are samplers, wall hangings and painted textiles, which in some cases can be construed as works of art.

The majority of textiles are woven (that is, with the longitudinal warp threads interlaced by transverse weft threads), but there are also knitted, crocheted, knotted and braided textiles, all of which have special qualities that appeal to collectors.

We tend to think of antique textiles as being made from natural materials, such as cotton, linen, wool and silk – but synthetic fibres began to be used for manufacturing cloth from around the turn of the century.

CLEANING TEXTILES

Cleaning not only improves the appearance of most antique textiles, it also removes soiling, which is often the catalyst for deterioration. Consequently, even very old and fragile items may need cleaning for their own protection, although this should only be done by experts.

Since items are often constructed from a number of different fabrics, it is important to examine them carefully before deciding on the best method of cleaning. This is not always as straightforward as it might seem, and you may have to get advice from a trained conservator.

GETTING EXPERT ADVICE

There are excellent textile restorers who work for antique dealers, but they may not have the in-depth technical background of a trained conservator. If you have an item that needs cleaning but are unsure of the best way to go about it, a textile conservator is probably your best bet for reliable advice.

One way to track down expert help is to phone your local museum. Even if there is no conservation department on site, the museum staff are bound to hire private consultants and conservators from time to time and should be able to recommend one to you.

Alternatively, a museum may be able to put you in touch with an organization that has a register of conservators working in your area. You will probably be sent the names and addresses of three or four experts who are willing to furnish advice or even undertake the work for you.

You should not feel the slightest embarrassment about taking items that are not particularly valuable to a conservator. He or she will always give you a range of options, depending on what you can afford to have done. Even if that advice is to store the textile safely until you can do something more constructive, you will at least have the benefit of informed opinion upon which to base your decision.

Testing for fugitive dyes

Probably the most important decision you will have to make is whether you can safely wash an item in water. Wet cleaning is an irreversible process, so you have to be sure that you are not going to do more harm than good. Not only must you be sure that the piece is not going to shrink, but it is imperative to find out whether any part of the textile is coloured with a fugitive dye that is going to run when immersed in water. It is safest to assume that a dye will run until you have tested it – and that means checking every colour separately, including the dyes used for trimmings and linings, embroidery cottons, and even patches and threads that may have been used for previous restoration. If there is the slightest indication that the textile contains fibres coloured with fugitive dyes, then don't wash the piece in water. Solvent cleaning is a possibility, but it should only be undertaken by a qualified conservator.

Testing individual samples

The most accurate method is to test a sample thread from every part of the piece you want to clean. Using tweezers and sharp nail scissors, trim a 3mm (⅛in) length of thread from a hem, the inside of a pocket, a long tail end of an embroidery cotton, or anywhere that can't be seen and where you won't damage the piece.

For the test, sandwich the sample threads between a pair of transparent glass weights. You can either buy these from a conservators' supplier, or get a glazier to cut two 100 x 40mm (4 x 1½in) pieces of glass 3mm (⅛in) thick and polish off the sharp edges.

1 Mounting the samples
Place a piece of blotting paper on one of the glass weights and lay your sample threads on the paper. If you have samples of a similar colour, label them for identification.

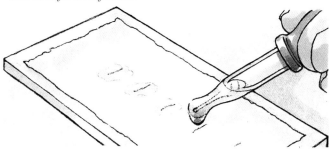

2 Wetting the samples
Make up a solution using the same proportion of soap and water as you intend to use for washing the piece. Using a dropper or an artist's paintbrush, deposit a small drop of solution onto each sample thread.

3 Applying the second weight
Put the other weight on top of the samples and monitor them for a few hours to see if any colour migrates into the blotting paper.

Testing with a cotton-wool bud
Although testing individual samples is preferable, you may not be able to find a thread end you can remove without harming the textile. Instead, barely moisten a cotton-wool bud with soap solution (see page 114) and touch it lightly against the surface of the cloth. You should only make this test on the inside of a hem or on a seam that is normally hidden – and don't attempt it on anything valuable. If you detect colour on the surface of the bud or on blotting paper pressed against the cloth, don't wash the item in water.

Be aware that some dyes take time before they run – which is why monitoring a variety of individual thread samples over a period of hours constitutes a more accurate test.

Washing textiles

Even when you are confident that the colour will not run, you still need to identify the fabric in order to know how it is likely to react when soaked in water. If in doubt, look for a manufacturer's label or seek expert advice.

Cotton and linen are generally safe to wash, but be wary about wetting wool. It reacts poorly to hot water, and any abrasion is likely to cause 'felting'. Don't wash rayon or early viscose; nor put mixed-fibre textiles in water, as they are liable to differential drying and shrinkage.

It is not a good idea to wash beaded items, wall hangings or large heavy garments; and never wash very fragile or valuable textiles yourself. Have all of these cleaned by a conservator.

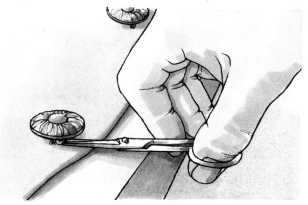

Removing buttons and fastenings
Before you put textiles in water, be sure to remove any buttons or fastenings made with metal components and check that there are no metallic threads woven into the piece that might cause rust staining. Also, remove any collectable buttons that could be harmed by immersion in water. It is worth noting that professional conservators retain the thread used to attach buttons or fastenings as evidence of historic construction.

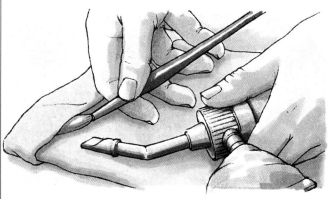

Removing loose dust and grit
Before you wash anything, always vacuum it first to remove grit and harmful particles trapped in the weave of the textile. If you fail to remove them, the water may drive these impurities deeper into the fibres.

Dust tends to collect in cuffs, turn-ups and pockets. Remove it with a soft brush and a vacuum-suction unit (see page 116). Check first that there are no small objects of interest left in the pockets.

Washing clothing

Provided they are in reasonable condition, cotton shirts and blouses, christening dresses and white cotton underwear are the kind of garments you can usually wash safely by hand. It is possible to support holes and worn areas with white nylon net to prevent them fraying while the piece is washed and dried – but it is not advisable to immerse any garment that shows signs of general deterioration. Never wash old textiles in a washing machine.

Remember to vacuum the garment before you wash it. Also, make sure you have everything you need to hand before putting the item in water.

Mixing a soap solution

Some textiles will benefit from soaking in water only, but ingrained soiling is likely to have been contaminated by grease particles that cannot be removed without some form of detergent. Unfortunately, however, the majority of modern detergents contain so many additives (bleaches, brighteners, enzymes) that they are potentially harmful to antique textiles. It is therefore safest to use only pure soap flakes recommended for washing woollens. Never use perfumed or coloured soaps – nor washing-up liquid – to wash old textiles.

Any soap that you use has to be rinsed out, so it makes sense to use as little as possible. The ideal concentration is 20g (¾oz) of soap flakes to 1 litre (1¾ pints) of water. The easiest method is to measure out the amount of water you need into a bowl or bath tub, then calculate the amount of soap you require to achieve the ideal concentration. Don't expect to generate foam – unless the water is extremely soft, foam indicates that there is too much soap in the solution.

Hot water can be very damaging, so always use lukewarm water – about 20–25°C (68–77°F). Ideally you should use soft water for washing and rinsing, changing to de-ionized water for the final rinse. A domestic filtration system that removes earth metals (magnesium, calcium and aluminium) is an advantage. You could wash small items in distilled water, or boil tap water and let it cool down before you use it.

As a last resort, run water into the bath and leave it for about 20 minutes to allow the chlorine to evaporate. Do the same between rinses.

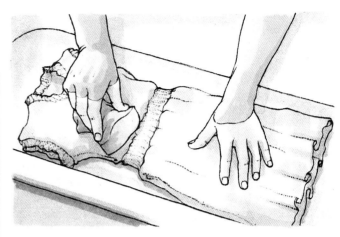

1 Sponging the garment
Lower the garment into the water and arrange it so that it lies as flat as possible. Leave it to soak for about 10 minutes, then dab it all over with a sponge to disturb the dirt. Don't squeeze or rub the fabric vigorously. Turn it over carefully and sponge the other side.

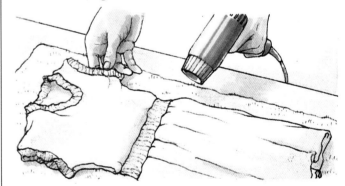

2 Rinsing in clean water
Gather up the garment in two hands and carefully lift it out of the dirty water. Refill the bath with fresh water and replace the garment, sponging it gently all over – rinse in two or three changes of water. If there are any bubbles or the fabric has an iridescent sheen, rinse again.

As a final test, take a small sample of water from the last rinse in a glass tumbler, place your hand over the top of the tumbler and shake the water vigorously. If any bubbles appear, rinse the item once more then test the water again.

3 Drying flat
Blot the garment between dry white towels to remove excess water. Because heat accelerates the deterioration of antique textiles, conservators never iron old fabrics. Instead, lay the rinsed garment flat on a thick white towel in a well-ventilated room to dry naturally, or use an electric fan or a hair dryer to blow cold air across the piece while you smooth out the creases by hand.

Preserving the shape

Fabrics invariably change shape when they take up water and often have to be eased back into shape as they dry, particularly when a piece has to be returned to a frame. However, for most people it is difficult to recall the exact proportions of an object unless they have a template for comparison.

1 Taking a tracing

Lay two layers of transparent acetate or polyester over the item that you are going to wash, and trace its outline with a fibre-tip pen. The double layer is merely a precaution against the point of the pen puncturing the acetate and marking the textile with ink.

2 Making a drying board

Cut a sheet of softboard larger than the textile; paste onto it a sheet of squared paper to help align the grain (warp and weft) of the fabric. Place the tracing on top, then wrap the board in transparent polyethylene.

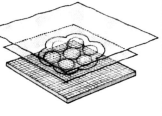

3 Drying the textile

Wash and rinse the textile, then lay it flat on the plastic-covered board to dry. The shape of the wet textile will no doubt be quite different from your tracing. As you dry the fabric with a cold hair dryer or a fan, gradually ease it back into shape, using the graph paper and tracing as a guide. Avoid stretching the fabric.

Supporting delicate textiles

Textiles are particularly vulnerable when wet because they can tear under their own weight. Consequently you need to support delicate textiles on a piece of fine nylon netting when washing them.

Cut the netting larger than the textile, so that you can hold it in two hands when lowering the piece into the water and when taking it out again. It is convenient to wash small items in a photographer's plastic tray.

Washing and drying delicate textiles

Wash and rinse the textile as described opposite, supporting it on the netting (see below left) each time you lift it out to change the water. Leave the textile on its support to dry flat on a clean towel or a polyethylene-covered board. Alternatively, leave the piece to dry naturally on a drying rack made from soft cotton net stretched over a frame.

Supporting weaker areas of the fabric

Prior to washing any piece of antique textile, examine it carefully for weak areas that may need supporting before it is immersed in water. It helps to tack a patch of white nylon net over holes or frayed edges – but get expert advice if the textile appears to be in a very fragile condition.

REMOVING STAINS

It is natural to want to remove disfiguring stains from antique textiles; since ingrained soiling is very likely to be acidic, it is probably also advantageous in terms of conservation. Nevertheless, lifting heavy soiling is not always entirely beneficial.

The main problem is identifying the nature of a stain in order to select the appropriate solvent. If the wrong solvent is applied, it can make removal doubly difficult – and many old stains prove to be permanent. Accurate identification can be tricky even for professional restorers, so do not hesitate to seek the advice of a trained textile conservator.

Secondly, you would not want to reduce the value of a piece by removing a stain that is part of its history. For example, cleaning a soiled uniform that has been worn in battle could eradicate all clues to its provenance and greatly reduce its interest to collectors and historians. Some form of cleaning may be necessary if the stains are harming the uniform; but, again, it is advisable to get an informed opinion before taking action.

In short, removing old stains may well do more harm than good – and it is always wisest to obtain expert advice before you proceed.

Dealing with mildew

If textiles have been stored in damp conditions, mildew staining may be evident. Wet cleaning will probably drive the soiling deeper into the fibres of the textile, so your best option is to allow the fabric to dry thoroughly, then try removing the mildew with vacuum suction and a sable brush (see page 116). If that doesn't work, take the piece to a professional.

Rust stains

Rusty fastenings can stain fabrics. This is a condition that needs treatment because it will eventually weaken the textile. However, do not be tempted to bleach the fabric; take it to a conservator for a professional opinion.

See also Emergency measures (page 120).

DRY-CLEANING METHODS

The chemicals used by ordinary high-street dry-cleaners are not suitable for antique clothes and textiles. However, there are specialists who are able to dry-clean older pieces that cannot be washed in water. Professional textile conservators are also trained in dry-cleaning methods.

Provided the piece is not heavily soiled, you can remove a noticeable amount of dust and dirt using vacuum suction.

Vacuum cleaning

Removing dust with vacuum suction is the safest way to clean old textiles, provided the piece is not fragile. However, most domestic vacuum cleaners are too powerful for conserving textiles, unless they are fitted with a dial that reduces the suction. Conservators' suppliers stock adapters that reduce the suction level of ordinary machines, and you can buy suitable battery-operated vacuum-suction units from similar sources. Even when using a reduced-suction vacuum cleaner, hold the nozzle just above the surface of the textile – never in contact with the fabric.

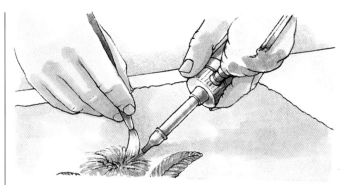

Cleaning embroidery
When extracting dust from embroidery, smocking or any textile of a three-dimensional nature, brush it gently with an artist's sable brush while holding the nozzle of the vacuum-suction unit close to the tip of the brush.

A makeshift filter
To prevent loose threads, small fastenings or beadwork being drawn into the cleaner, stretch a piece of fine white nylon net over the nozzle and secure it with an elastic band.

Always examine beaded textiles carefully before vacuum cleaning, to make sure the beads are held in place with sound threads. Use a cotton bud barely moistened with distilled water to remove greasy deposits from the surface of the beads.

Cleaning metallic threads
Metallic threads used to make epaulettes, frogging and military insignia can become badly tarnished. Surface-clean with vacuum suction, then take a cotton bud barely moistened with distilled water and dab the surface of the threads. The effect may not be dramatic, but if you examine the surface of the bud you will see how much dirt is being removed. Don't attempt to remove tarnish with metal polish.

MAKING MINOR REPAIRS

Repairs to valuable textiles and historical costume should be left to a conservator, but there are a great many items sold in antique markets and second-hand-clothing stores that need only a few minor repairs to give them a new lease of life.

Don't attempt to replace worn embroidery or missing beadwork with modern materials. It is better to live with old textiles that are less than perfect, rather than risk reducing their value or appearance through inappropriate restoration.

Also be aware of 'historical' wear. Worn cuffs and button holes are only to be expected in a garment that has seen fair wear and tear, and detract little from its appeal. You may even find that a collar has been 'turned' at some time in the past in order to prolong the useful life of a well-worn garment. That too is an interesting clue to its past history, and you would be best advised to leave it alone unless the old repair is actually causing damage to the costume.

On the other hand, sewing up a loose hem or patching a torn sleeve can do little harm – and you may end up tearing the garment if you don't make repairs of this kind at the earliest opportunity.

An approach to repairing textiles

Before deciding what to do with any damaged textile, try to determine what is likely to be the future role of the piece in question.

If it is to be mounted for display only, you might choose to do little more than arrest present deterioration. If, on the other hand, you intend to use or wear a particular item, then you will probably want to undertake repairs that allow the piece to function reasonably well, at the same time protecting it from unnecessary damage. For example, you would no doubt want to replace broken or missing fastenings before wearing an article of period clothing – and it is worth patching a small hole in a tablecloth before someone accidentally converts the hole into a tear.

Any textile in a fragile condition should be examined by an expert before you attempt to make even small repairs. Weak textiles may require full support before they can be displayed, and that is a job best left to a professional who can ensure that the weight of the textile is carried by the support, and not the other way round.

There are few hard-and-fast rules to guide you – except that any repair should be reversible (so never use adhesives to mend antique textiles) and, if you need to repair something you care about deeply, have it restored by a conservator unless you have complete confidence in your own ability.

Choosing sympathetic materials

Any expert will tell you that if you are going to repair old textiles you should always use materials that are sympathetic to the item you are restoring. However, that advice can be interpreted in different ways.

One school of thought says you should always choose like for like – so that, by using identical materials, you ensure that old and new will react in harmony and age at a similar rate. However, common sense tells you that there may be little point in repairing a silk textile with a comparatively weak silk thread, when a stranded embroidery cotton would make for a repair that will last longer and therefore save the textile from unnecessary handling and stress in the future.

In order to achieve sympathetic repairs, try to find fabrics that are identical in colour and similar to the original article in weight and density of weave.

Needles

When you are making stitched repairs, it is important to select an appropriate needle for the fabric you are restoring. Perhaps the most vital factor is size. If, for example, you are sewing a fine silk or a cotton lawn, choose a very fine needle to avoid leaving holes in the fabric. Embroidery needles are ideal because they have very sharp points. Some conservators like to use exceptionally fine beading needles when repairing delicate fabrics. Discard blunt needles, which will damage the weave.

Curved needles are often required for mounting textiles on a fabric-covered board. If you can't find one the right size, improvise by bending a straight needle.

Fine sewing threads

When patching very fine fabrics, it can be a problem to find equally fine sewing threads that are strong enough. You might try using cotton lace-making yarn, which you can buy from most haberdashers. You could also use crewel wool, polyester, silk or mercerized-cotton threads. Some conservators go to the trouble of drawing a thread out of a piece of fine woven polyester fabric; the drawn thread is as fine as a human hair, and practically invisible when stitched into a repair.

PATCHING DAMAGED TEXTILES

Never sew up the edges of a torn textile, nor darn holes. The stitching will inevitably put strain on the surrounding fabric and probably make matters even worse. Always patch both tears and holes to support the weakened fabric, especially if the item is to be worn or hung. However, the tension must be just right if the patch is not to cause further damage – a badly applied patch is likely to cause more problems than it solves.

1 Cutting the patch
Select an appropriate support fabric for the repair and cut out a patch, using pinking shears. Make the patch large enough to ensure the edges can be sewn into the stronger areas of the textile – not just into the relatively weak fabric around the tear itself.

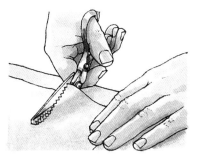

2 Arranging the torn edges
Before you apply the patch, arrange the torn fabric so that the warp and weft threads are aligned correctly and as straight as possible. Allow the torn edges to butt against each other but not overlap. Smooth down any frayed edges so that the cloth is lying flat.

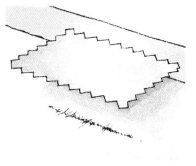

Mending torn fabric
Although patches are always applied to the back of the textile, you work from the front with your support stitches visible on the face of the textile. This is why the sewing thread must be as fine as is practicable and also a good colour match. Working from the front allows you to see exactly what you are doing, and lets you monitor the progress of the repair.

Since it is particularly difficult to patch three-dimensional textiles, such as puff sleeves or bonnets, take these to an expert for repair.

3 Pinning the patch in place
Pin the patch to the back of the textile, using fine straight pins. Check that the torn edges are still butted neatly together.

4 Inserting the laid thread
Torn fabric is repaired with laid couching stitches, applied at 90 degrees to the tear and running from one strong area of the fabric to the other.

To make the first laid thread, bring your threaded needle up on one side, then take the thread in a straight line across the tear and down through the fabric again.

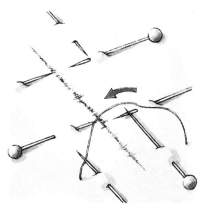

5 Couching the thread
Bring the needle back up next to the laid thread, about 3mm (⅛in) from where it last entered the fabric. Take the needle over the laid thread and back through the fabric to form a small couching stitch that anchors the laid thread in place.

6 Completing a row of couching stitches
Continue to make similar couching stitches at 3mm (⅛in) intervals along the laid thread.

7 Continuing with support stitches
Insert a second laid thread about 3mm (⅛in) to one side, parallel with the one you have just couched, and anchor it with couching stitches. Continue with laid couching stitches along the entire length of the tear.

8 Sewing the edges of the patch
If the patch is larger than about 65mm (2½in) square, secure its edges to the textile with herringbone stitches. There is no need to sew the edges of smaller patches.

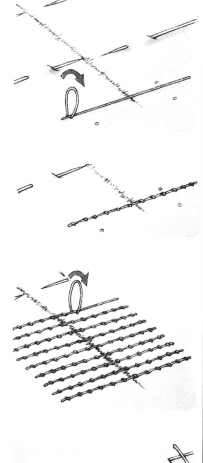

Patching a hole
Proceed with patching a hole, using the method described for repairing torn cloth, but use staggered long-and-short stitches to secure the edges of the hole to the patch.

REPLACING BUTTONS AND FASTENINGS

Although it may be difficult to find an exact replacement for a single missing button or fastening, it is fairly easy to track down a set of genuine period buttons to complement, say, a Victorian dress or a 1930s overcoat. Antique buttons are collector's items, so check their value or rarity before wearing them. Don't cut buttons off an original show card, as that is collectable too.

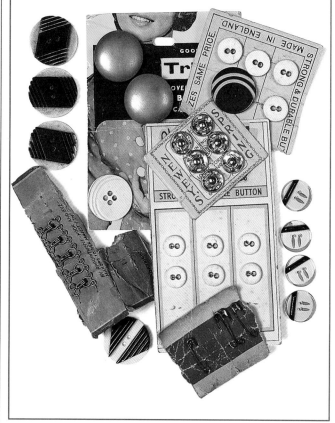

Securing loose beads

Examine antique beadwork carefully to see if any of the threads that hold the beads in place have broken.

Sewing individual beads
If possible, ascertain the type of stitching that was used originally and copy it when securing loose beads. If in doubt, cast on the thread as close to the bead as possible, secure the bead with two stitches and then cast off the thread, leaving a long thread end.

Securing a row of beads
Quite often beads were threaded onto a single thread that was then sewn onto the backing fabric. As a result, if one bead works loose you could lose the entire row. To prevent that happening, secure the row of beads with couching stitches and oversew the loose thread end to anchor it to the fabric.

USING AND STORING TEXTILES

The majority of items in most antique-textile collections are rarely put out on display, simply because they don't lend themselves to convenient presentation. But there are exceptions, such as wall hangings, samplers and other embroideries – all of which have similarities to pictures and other two-dimensional works of art. Decorated pincushions, fabric-covered shoes or beaded purses can be housed in glass-fronted display cases, but few collectors have room to exhibit items such as period costume; most are therefore primarily concerned with how to keep their collections safe from deterioration. Also, when clothing, tablecloths and other collectable items are put to use, accessible storage tends to take priority over display.

Wearing antique clothing

Fashion revivals fuel a brisk trade in old clothes that suddenly become wearable; and heirlooms such as wedding gowns and christening dresses are often handed down to be worn by succeeding generations. There's an obvious risk of accidental damage when you wear period clothing – so inspect each piece carefully and, even more important, have it cleaned before putting it back into store. Simple cotton or linen garments can be washed by hand (see page 114), but it's best to have more complex items cleaned by specialist dry-cleaners. Although relatively expensive compared with high-street cleaners, they have experience of handling delicate textiles.

Emergency measures

No matter how careful you are, there is always the possibility of spilling something that will stain clothing or domestic linen. Although most stained items should be taken to a specialist cleaner as soon as possible, it pays to take emergency measures to minimize the damage.

There is no guarantee that they will work – but, since the damage is already done, there is little to lose.

● **Red wine**
To neutralize the effect of spilling red wine, immediately pour white wine onto the stain. Alternatively, if you have washed the piece successfully in the past, leave it to soak in cold water.

For textiles that cannot be wet-cleaned, pour a generous pile of salt onto the stain and leave it to absorb the wine. The next day, remove the salt with vacuum suction.

● **Strawberry or raspberry jam**
If you know a tablecloth is safe to wash, soak jam stains in very hot water.

● **Candle wax**
If candle wax drips onto a tablecloth or napkins, pick off the hardened lumps, then cover the stain with brown parcel paper, shiny-side up. Press the paper with a warm domestic iron to melt the wax and draw it out of the fabric. Repeat the process with clean paper until all the wax is removed.

● **Perspiration stains**
Perspiration stains are virtually impossible to remove, especially from silk and synthetic fibres. Specialist dry-cleaning with solvents may have an effect – but the chances are slim.

● **Ink**
Blot up as much of the ink as possible and take the damaged item to a textile conservator without delay.

● **Mud**
Let mud dry, then gently brush it off while using vacuum suction (see page 116). Never attempt to remove mud while it is still wet.

● **Saturation**
A burst pipe or a flood is potentially disastrous for antique textiles. If you allow them to dry out, any water staining may become permanent. Wrap saturated textiles in polyethylene and put them in a freezer, then take them to a conservator as soon as possible.

Storing textiles

Antique textiles should be stored in the dark to protect them from the effects of ultra-violet light. A dry, cool environment is also essential.

Wrapping in tissue paper
Ideally, textiles should be wrapped in acid-free tissue paper and stored flat in strong acid-free cardboard boxes. If you have to fold textiles for storage, pad each fold with a roll of tissue paper to prevent it becoming a permanent crease.

Storing flat textiles on tubes
Roll larger pieces, face side out, on an acid-free cardboard tube or PVC drainage pipes covered with tissue paper. Make sure the grain is straight and, if possible, roll the textile in the direction of the warps.

Lay more sheets of paper on top of the textile as you begin to roll it onto the tube. Secure the roll with white-cotton tape or, better still, wrap it in a sheet of washed calico.

Storing clothing
You can store old clothes in acid-free cardboard boxes as described above, but make sure you pad sleeves, bodices and folds with tissue paper.

To prevent metal buttons staining the fabric, cut 'button holes' in small squares of acid-free tissue paper and slip them over the buttons.

Nothing you do will prevent silver buttons tarnishing if they are sewn to a woollen garment. Metallic threadwork found on military uniforms may be affected similarly and, although a conservator can clean it for you, the metal will tarnish again after a relatively short period.

Before putting items of clothing into store, remove any pins or brooches attached to them.

Storing accessories
Pad hats and shoes with acid-free tissue to help them keep their shape. Store them in cardboard archival boxes with metal-reinforced corners. Protect evening bags and purses in a similar way, making sure they are not piled one on top of the other in storage.

Hanging garments
Hang larger garments from padded coat hangers and cover them with calico bags, tied at the bottom with tape. Don't use plastic bags – they attract dust and encourage mould growth.

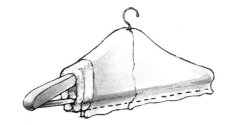

Padding a coat hanger
Choose a strong coat hanger, preferably one that has a straight trouser rail and which fits the shoulder width of the garment you are storing.

Wrap the coat hanger in polyester wadding – the type used for making quilts – which is available from any department store. Ensure the padding is adequate for the shoulders and to support the upper part of the garment, if need be adding a second layer of wadding. Stitch through the wadding with white cotton thread to hold it in place, then cover it with washed calico.

If required, you can extend the wadding below the coat hanger and shape it with scissors to pad out the bodice of a dress.

Sewing loops to the waistband
In order to suspend a skirt from a coat hanger, sew wide cotton-tape loops to the waistband – one at the front, one at the back, and one at each side.

Hang a heavy beaded dress, or dresses that are delicate or weak, from similar tapes that take the strain off the bodice. Run the tapes up from the waistband to support the weight of the skirt on the hanger.

PROTECTING TEXTILES FROM MOTHS

Moths sometimes lay their eggs on silk, but are particularly attracted to the sulphur that is present in wool. When the larvae hatch, they feed on the fibres of the textile, leaving the characteristic ragged holes.

To protect your collection from infestation, make sure the textiles themselves are clean before you store them, and dust or vacuum the insides of cupboards, drawers and wardrobes.

Rub cedar oil into the inside of wooden drawers and wardrobes (you can obtain it from anywhere that sells aromatherapy oils). Cedar oil not only keeps moths at bay but fills the space with an attractive scent.

No textile conservator would ever advocate the use of moth balls – naphthalene can be a health risk under certain circumstances.

Eradicating moths
If you discover live moths in your wardrobe or detect signs of infestation, wrap all the stored textiles in plastic bags and take them outside where you can brush and vacuum them to remove remaining insect eggs. Make sure you vacuum seams, pockets and turn-ups thoroughly. As a precaution, clean all the garments in the wardrobe and consider having them fumigated by an expert.

Freezing is a sure way of eradicating infestation, but you need to wrap the textiles in polyethylene and leave them for a week in a freezer that can be set to a temperature of minus 20°C (4°F). Unless you have access to an industrial freezer, ask the conservation department at your local museum to recommend someone who has a suitable facility. Vacuum the textiles after they have thawed out.

DISPLAYING TEXTILES

Antique textiles make delightful wall hangings, but they need to be mounted and displayed with care in order to protect them from damage. Museums display textiles in low levels of light that are impractical at home, but since you need to protect your collection from damaging levels of ultra-violet light never hang textiles in direct sunlight or illuminate them with spotlights. Net curtains or half-drawn blinds help reduce daylight to an acceptable level, and it is worth drawing the curtains in rooms that are not used during the day.

Textiles will be harmed if you hang them above a source of heat, such as a radiator or open fire. Heated rising air makes fibres brittle and deposits dust onto unprotected textiles.

Don't hang textiles on outside walls that suffer from penetrating damp or condensation.

Like drawings and prints, ideally antique textiles should be mounted behind glass – but if you have a wall hanging that is too large for framing, suspend it from a batten to distribute the weight evenly, thus reducing strain on the weaker areas of the textile.

Framing textiles

Small embroidered samplers and delicate pieces of lace can be framed like pictures, but it is worth discussing your plans with a conservator in case there is something about your item that is unusual or might prove difficult to handle.

Amateurs can safely mount textiles that are about the size of a man's handkerchief. Anything larger, especially if it is fragile, is best left to a professional who has done this type of work before.

Choosing a frame

Don't use ready-made picture frames for displaying antique textiles. Since the piece is to be sealed behind glass, it is imperative that all the materials used to construct the frame are inert, otherwise they may harm the textile over a period of time. An experienced framer or a textile conservator will advise you to steer clear of frames made from pine, oak or mahogany. You should also seal the inner face of the frame's backing board to prevent acids leaching into the fibres of the textile. Professionals tend to use an iron-on foil sheet which you can buy from a conservators' supplier.

The surface of the textile should not be allowed to touch the glass – so make sure the rabbet in the frame is deep enough for a narrow fillet, or use a thick window mount cut from acid-free card (see pages 24–5).

Mounting textiles

Before they are framed, antique textiles should be supported on a padded board. Make the mounting board from acid-free cardboard and cotton domette, covered with a fabric – linen or cotton is a good choice – that compliments the antique textile. Wash the covering fabric in hot water, without adding detergent, to ensure that it is preshrunk before being mounted and to remove the manufacturer's dressing. Dry and iron the fabric. Similarly, wash the cotton domette in warm water.

1 Making the mounting board
To make a mounting board that will stay flat, glue together two sheets of acid-free cardboard, with the grain of each board running at 90 degrees to the other. Use water-based PVA adhesive. Cut the finished board at least 18mm (¾in) larger all round than the textile that is to be mounted, in order to create a handling edge.

2 Padding the mounting board
Cut a piece of cotton domette about 75mm (3in) larger all round than the mounting board. Place the board in the centre of the domette so that it aligns accurately with the warp and weft threads. Holding the board down firmly with one hand, fold the edges of the fabric over and secure them with glass-headed pins driven into the edges of the cardboard.

3 Adjusting the tension
To check that the tension is adequate, lay the padded board face up on a worktop and run the tip of your finger firmly up the centre of the board. If the domette ripples, take up the excess by removing the pins and putting a little more tension on the fabric. If the board buckles, release tension on the domette.

Adjust the tension across the width of the board the same way.

4 Gluing the domette
Lay the board face down again and paint a strip of PVA glue around the perimeter of the card. Fold the edges of the domette over and rub them down onto the glue, cutting mitres at each corner so that the fabric will lie flat. Let the glue set and remove the pins.

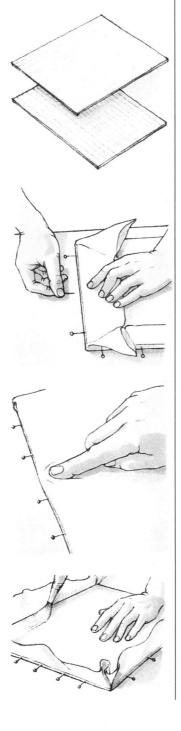

5 Mounting the covering fabric
Cut out a piece of fabric 25 to 50mm (1 to 2in) larger all round than the domette. Stretch it over the padded board (see left), then check that the tension is adequate and glue the fabric onto the back of the board. Make sure the warp and weft threads are parallel with the edges of the card, then cut mitres at each corner. Leave the glue to set.

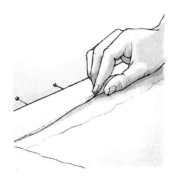

6 Aligning the textile
It helps to set up a temporary guide for mounting the textile sample on the board. This is especially useful when mounting asymmetrical samples. Insert straight pins into the edges of the board, equidistant from each corner. Lightly stretch cotton threads from pin to pin across the board.

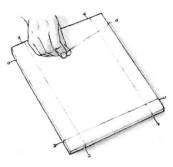

7 Pinning the textile in place
Having carried out any repairs required to conserve the textile, lay it centrally onto the fabric-covered board and pin it in place with a straight glass-headed pin driven through each corner into the card. Add other pins as need be to tension the textile firmly, but don't stretch it. Make sure the grain of the textile aligns with that of the covering fabric.

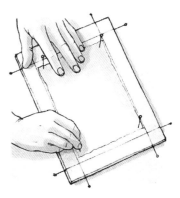

8 Stitching the textile to the fabric
Using a fine curved needle, sew the textile to the backing fabric with herringbone stitches. Sew across the top edge, down the sides, then across the bottom, gradually removing the pins as the work progresses.

Cast off with two small stitches, pass the needle back through the line of herringbone stitches for about 25mm (1in), then cut off the thread.

Finally, mount the textile in the frame and tape the back to seal out dust (see pages 24–5).

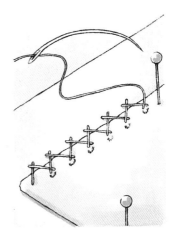

Hanging larger textiles

To display textiles too large to mount behind glass, attach them to a linen or cotton-downproof lining and suspend the lining from a wall-hung batten. Wash the lining to remove the manufacturer's dressing. Then dry and iron it flat, ensuring that the grain of the fabric is not distorted.

Get a professional to line any textile larger than 1 metre (1 yard) square.

Attaching the lining

On all sides, the finished lining should be 6mm (¼in) smaller than the textile. When measuring the fabric for the lining, include an extra 10mm (⅜in) for every 300mm (1ft) across the width and from top to bottom. This excess fabric will ensure that the textile will not buckle should the lining contract for any reason. In addition, allow for a 30mm (1¼in) fold on all four edges of the lining.

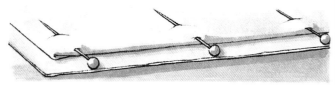

Pinning the lining to the textile
Lay the textile face down, aligned with the front edge of the worktop. Fold the edges of the lining fabric under and pin it to the textile – each folded edge should be 6mm (¼in) from the edge of the textile. Use glass-headed pins spaced 40mm (1½in) apart. As you pin the lining in place, gradually take up the excess fabric.

Using a lining stitch

A lining stitch holds the lining close to the textile, preventing the ingress of insects and dust particles.

1 Inserting the needle into the folded edge
To make each stitch, insert the needle into the folded edge of the lining and let the point emerge 10mm (⅜in) further along. Pass the needle down through the textile beside the hole from which the thread emerges from the folded edge of the lining.

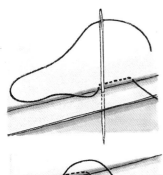

2 Back stitching
Pass the needle back up through the textile 1mm (1/32in) to the right, then insert the point of the needle into the same hole in the folded edge of the lining.

3 Putting tension on the stitch
Let the point of the needle emerge 10mm (⅜in) further along the folded edge, then pull on the thread to bring the lining close to the textile. Make a similar lining stitch at that point.

Using hook-and-loop tape
Having stitched the lining to the textile on all four sides, attach the hanging to a wall-hung batten, using peel-off Velcro hook-and-loop tape.

1 Sewing the tape to the hanging
Using a relatively thick polyester thread, sew the softer half of the tape along the top edge of the lining. Use V-shape stitches, about 6mm (¼in) long, that pass right through lining and textile. Don't machine-stitch the tape to the hanging.

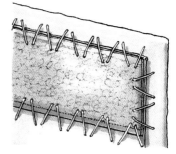

2 Stapling the tape to the batten
Screw the batten to the wall and attach the other half of the tape to the batten with strong upholsterer's staples.

3 Mounting the hanging on the batten
Get someone to help you mount the hanging on the batten. One method is to roll the hanging and begin attaching it at one end of the batten. Press the two halves of the Velcro tape together, while your assistant supports the weight of the hanging and unrolls it as you proceed.

Alternatively, mark the centre of the batten, place the midpoint of the hanging on that mark, and work outwards from the centre. You may need two assistants for this method.

Once the hanging is attached to the batten, you can make any minor adjustments necessary.

RUGS AND CARPETS

A great many machine-made rugs and carpets are attractive as well as durable, but collectors are almost invariably drawn to hand-woven or knotted-pile rugs. Though a rather specialized form of textile, all rugs are basically warp-and-weft based. In terms of manufacture the flat-woven kilims and sumaks are hardly distinguishable from other woven textiles, but knotted-pile rugs and carpets are made in a significantly different manner.

Making knotted-pile rugs

Wool or sometimes silk yarn is tied in a knot around pairs of parallel warp threads that run from the top of the loom to the bottom. Having completed a row of knots, the weaver introduces transverse weft threads that are beaten down with a comb to hold the knots securely to the foundation threads. After each knot is tied, the yarn is severed with a knife; and when the row is complete, the knot ends are trimmed to length with scissors, forming a short tufted pile.

As the work progresses, the weaver introduces yarns of various colours to create the pattern of the rug. Being handmade, often by nomadic peoples who have to dismantle the loom frequently, the pattern of oriental rugs is rarely regular or symmetrical and the colour of the yarns can vary considerably – but far from detracting from their value, it is these variations that give antique rugs their special appeal and charm.

A comparatively narrow flat-woven strip at each end of the rug protects the knotted pile and, together with the fringe, forms a decorative border. The fringes are made from the warp threads that have been cut from the loom, and are sometimes knotted to form long tassels.

TYPES OF KNOT

The type of knots used to make rugs varies according to local tradition. The two most common types are the Turkish or Ghiordes knot and the asymmetric Persian or Senneh knot. The Turkish Jufti knot is similar to the Ghiordes knot, but it is tied around four foundation warps instead of the usual two.

Owing to the movement of various tribes and peoples in the past, it is impossible to be absolutely categorical about where these different knots were used, but in the main the Ghiordes knot derives from Turkey and from parts of western Iran and the Caucasus. The Persian Senneh knot is found in rugs made in Iran, India and China.

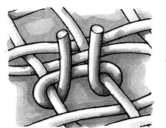

TURKISH OR GHIORDES KNOT

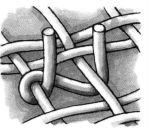

PERSIAN OR SENNEH KNOT

JUFTI KNOT

CLEANING RUGS AND CARPETS

Rugs and carpets need cleaning regularly to prevent infestation by moths and carpet beetles, and to remove minute particles of grit that wear away at the fibres. Although vacuum suction is the norm for cleaning modern floorcoverings, it is unwise to use an ordinary domestic vacuum cleaner on antique rugs and carpets, especially if they are in a fragile condition – since, as soon as a rug begins to wear, powerful suction can pull it to pieces. Unless you are prepared to invest in a museum-quality low-suction vacuum cleaner, it is therefore much safer to remove dust and dirt from knotted carpets and kilims with a soft-bristle brush. This is also the method recommended for cleaning any silk rug.

Try to brush your floorcoverings once a week, and consult an oriental-rug specialist about the advisability of having them cleaned every couple of years. Once a month, lift a rug or carpet so that you can sweep up the dirt from the floor beneath it and brush the back of the carpet.

Brushing carpets
Use a soft-bristle banister brush to clean antique carpets and rugs. Brush them gently by hand, only in the direction of the pile (from top to bottom).

Removing stains
Most people are prepared to live with a few minor stains, provided they are not too disfiguring. In any case, stains hardly show on colourful patterned rugs and carpets. However, it pays to have an expert identify an old stain for you, in case it is doing irreparable harm to the fibres of the rug. He or she will tell you whether it's worth removing and give you an estimate for doing the work. See also, pages 128–9.

DETECTING THE DIRECTION OF THE PILE

If you run your hand up and down the carpet, you'll find it feels smoother in one direction and rougher in the other. When brushing the carpet, work in the direction that feels smoothest, which avoids lifting the pile.

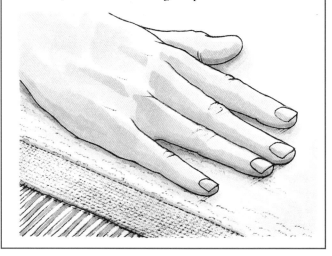

REPAIRING RUGS AND CARPETS

Nobody expects a rug that has been subjected to heavy foot traffic over the years to still be in perfect condition. Consequently, even very worn rugs may not require restoration unless they are in danger of serious deterioration.

Professional restorers perform minor miracles, including invisibly mending holes and worn patches. However, repairs of this kind demand skill and a practised eye able to match existing colours and re-create missing pattern. A restorer can also replace missing fringes and rebuild damaged side cords, work that is hard on the fingers and likely to damage the rug unless undertaken by an expert.

Nevertheless, you can avoid further deterioration by stopping your rug fraying and by making minor repairs before the damage becomes too severe.

Preventing a rug fraying

The kilim end, the narrow band of closely woven threads at each end of a piled rug, holds the knotted pile in place and prevents the rug unravelling. Once a kilim end begins to fray, prompt treatment is required to protect the main patterned area of the rug from damage.

Buy a strip of upholsterer's webbing tape made from unbleached cotton. They are available up to 50mm (2in) wide, so choose one that suits the width of the kilim ends. Most department stores stock this type of tape, or you may be able to get it from a good haberdasher.

If you need to match the colour of the kilim end, you can dye the tape with a cold-water dye.

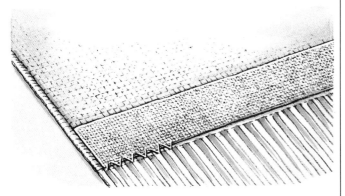

Attaching the tape
Sew the tape by hand to the kilim end, following the shape of the worn edge. Make V-shape stitches along both sides of the tape, using a relatively thick polyester thread. If the tape is slightly wider than you need, restrict both rows of stitches to the kilim end – don't sew the tape to the knotted pile.

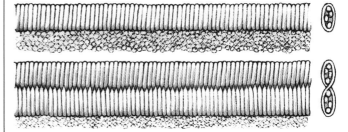

Repairing worn side cords

As part of the weaving process, weft threads are wound around the last few warp threads on each side of the carpet. When the rug is finished, the edges are bound with yarn to make strong side cords. Some carpets have double side cords, made with figure-of-eight binding.

Because they are thicker than the rest of the rug, the side cords wear relatively quickly. It pays to replace damaged binding before the warp and weft threads begin to wear.

1 Inserting new binding thread
Insert a threaded needle under the existing binding just where the damage begins. Let the point emerge about 12mm (½in) further along the cord.

2 Binding the edge
Working back from that point, oversew the damaged cord with neat closely packed stitches, – but don't pull the stitches too tight, or you will distort the line of the cord.

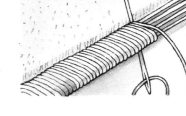

3 Tying off
Continue sewing 12mm (½in) beyond the worn section, then run the needle back through the new binding for about 25mm (1in) and cut off the yarn where it emerges.

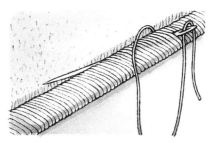

Using and displaying rugs

Perhaps more than most antiques, rugs and carpets are used for their original purpose. This makes them particularly vulnerable, since floorcoverings can deteriorate rapidly unless care is taken to reduce their exposure to wear and to prevent accidents.

Protecting rugs from damage
Avoid using old rugs and carpets in hallways, stairs or landings, and in other areas through which there is constant traffic. The dining room is one of the worst locations for floorcoverings. They not only have to bear the weight of the dining table, but scuffing from feet and chair legs is concentrated in a small area, and food and drink inevitably get spilled onto the floor. Even if you keep your antique rugs in bedrooms, where you are less likely to wear heavy shoes or boots, it pays to turn your rugs regularly to alleviate uneven wear and fading.

Don't place heavy furniture on an antique carpet. It is also advisable to use plastic furniture cups, to protect carpets from chair legs and castors.

Don't lay a rug or carpet directly onto a stone, tiled or concrete floor, or over floorboards with wide gaps between them. A good-quality underlay will reduce wear and prevents dust blowing between the boards, leaving dirty streaks on the surface of the floorcovering. A rug laid over a fitted carpet requires a double-sided underlay to prevent it moving on the pile below.

Plumbing leaks can be extremely damaging, especially those from central-heating systems that contain chemical descalers and corrosion inhibitors. Check your radiator valves regularly for leaks. Use an efficient fireguard to protect fireside rugs from sparks and falling coals.

RUGS AS WALL HANGINGS

Better-quality rugs and ones that are too worn to be laid on the floor can be used as wall hangings. However, they must be hung in such a way that their weight is distributed evenly, to avoid putting strain on weak areas. Don't hang rugs in direct sunlight or on damp walls, or over a fireplace or radiator.

Hanging a rug on a curtain pole
Make a sleeve from which to suspend the rug by stitching carpet-binding tape 50mm (2in) wide to the back of the rug, about 18mm (¾in) below the fringe or kilim end. Using strong polyester thread, sew along the top and bottom edges of the tape, allowing sufficient slack for the pole to pass though the sleeve.

Support each end of the pole on a wall bracket, or hang the pole from chains.

Using hook-and-loop tape
Use Velcro tape to support a heavy rug. Sew one half of the tape to the back of the rug, and staple the other half to a wall-hung batten (see page 124).

Emergency measures

If an antique rug is laid on the floor, you can be sure someone will spill something on it eventually. It is a risk we all take, but you may be able to prevent permanent staining if you act quickly. If emergency measures are unsuccessful, take the rug to a specialist for an expert opinion.

Mopping up spilled liquids
It is imperative to mop up spilled liquids immediately, to prevent them soaking deeply into rugs and carpets.

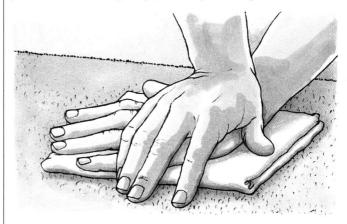

1 Using absorbent towels
Fold a dry white tea towel into a pad, lay it over the wet patch and apply firm pressure. Once the cloth is thoroughly wet, apply another dry cloth and apply pressure again. Continue in this way until all excess liquid appears to have been absorbed.

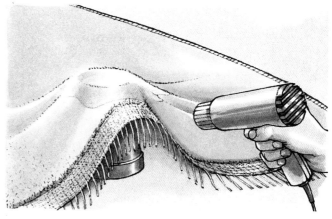

2 Drying the rug
If it is clean water that has been spilled, once you have mopped up the excess water dry the carpet with either a hair dryer at a cold setting or an electric fan. Try raising the wet section of the carpet in order to create better circulation. When the carpet is dry, fluff up the pile with your fingertips.

Absorbing red wine

Remove as much wine as possible with absorbent towels, then sprinkle a large heap of salt onto the patch. Next morning remove the salt.

Animal urine

Urine contains acid that is injurious to textiles. It may be tempting to wash out the urine with water, but washing may make matters worse.

Pick up a soiled rug immediately and either take it into the kitchen or put a sheet of plastic under the rug to protect the floor or floorcovering beneath.

Mop up as much liquid as possible with clean cotton rags, then take the rug to a conservator.

As a precaution, don't lay antique rugs or carpets in rooms where pets are allowed.

Removing mud

If someone treads mud across a carpet or rug, allow it to dry thoroughly then pick off as many lumps as possible before brushing off the remaining mud.

Removing chewing gum

To remove chewing gum that has been dropped on your carpet, put an ice cube in a plastic bag and hold it against the gum. When the gum has frozen hard, pick it off carefully with a blunt kitchen knife. However, if the carpet is valuable or particularly fragile, take it to a professional – don't try to treat it yourself.

STORING RUGS AND CARPETS

Leaving a rug folded for a long time will result in creases becoming permanent. If you have to put a rug into storage, roll it up on a length of large-diameter plastic pipe. Choose a tube that will project from each end of the carpet.

To avoid crushing the pile, always roll a knotted rug from the top. Run the palm of your hand back and forth along the rug – when the pile feels rough, your hand is moving towards the top of the rug.

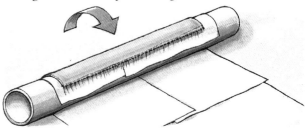

Rolling a rug
Lay the rug face down and cover it with acid-free tissue paper. Place the tube at the top of the rug and roll it up, smoothing down the pile as you go. Wrap the rolled rug in an old cotton sheet or a piece of washed calico and secure it with wide cotton tape.

If possible, support the ends of the tube to keep the rolled rug horizontal and off the ground – don't store rolled rugs on end.

Using antique rugs as floorcoverings
Use good-quality underlay when you lay antique rugs over floorboards, and protect the pile by putting furniture cups under the legs of a coffee table.

THE RAW MATERIALS

Plastic materials are those which at some stage of their manufacture are malleable and capable of being moulded. Although this broadly includes inorganic materials such as mortar or plaster, the term 'plastics' is generally used to describe natural and synthetic materials that have a polymeric structure. Polymers are large, long-chain molecules made up from many (in Greek, 'poly') parts.

Tortoiseshell and horn are naturally occurring organic plastic materials that can be moulded with heat and pressure. Early man-made plastics were produced by processing natural substances such as rubber, cellulose, tree resins, shellac and milk. Most plastics today, however, are based on synthetic polymers, typically derived from petrochemicals. They form an extensive range of materials, with distinctive properties that vary according to their individual composition and processing.

Plastics are broadly grouped into two categories, thermoplastics and thermosetting plastics (sometimes called thermosets). Thermoplastics can be returned to their fluid state with the application of heat. In contrast, thermosetting plastics are transformed by a chemical reaction when cured and cannot be reversed; the majority of them are also hard and brittle, unlike the wider range of thermoplastics.

PLASTICS

We live in an age of plastics, where we are constantly in contact with plastics in one form or another. Probably more than any other material, they have helped generate the throw-away society – for plastic products have become so familiar and inexpensive that we think nothing of disposing of them.

Plastic materials based on organic substances were developed in the mid nineteenth century. This early pioneering work led to the birth of a new industry that developed rapidly in the 1930s with the introduction of new synthetic materials – a situation that continues to this day. Plastics were first developed as a substitute for natural materials such as ivory, tortoiseshell and amber, but their versatility is so great that they were soon used to make products previously made from wood, metal, glass, ceramics, and even leather and cloth.

There is now a growing interest in old products made from plastics. However, despite modern claims that they are indestructible, all plastics will degrade. The chemical nature of plastics makes them susceptible to changes in the environment, and only time will tell which are the most durable. The information here briefly describes the most common plastics used to produce all manner of products up to the 1950s and gives basic information on how to care for them.

TYPES OF PLASTICS

The collector of plastic artefacts may choose to concentrate on a particular type of material or build up a collection based on objects that have other merits, such as subject matter, appearance or function. Whatever the focus of the collection, it is helpful to know the type of plastic used – not just for academic reasons, but also to establish the best means for conserving the material.

The services of a chemistry laboratory would be needed to determine the precise formulation of a particular plastic from the range of polymers and additives that make up the many different plastics used for commercial purposes. However, that is rarely necessary, and many of the clues required to broadly identify a type of plastic can be gleaned by observation, based on the surface texture, colour, opacity, hardness or softness, and smell. The period style and function of the object and the method of manufacture are also useful clues. If in doubt, take it to a specialist dealer or a relevant museum.

METHODS OF MANUFACTURE

Most plastics materials are liquefied and formed in a mould by the application of heat and pressure, although some are produced for cold casting.

Thermoplastics produced as sheet or rod can be readily bent or pressed into shape when reheated. Postforming, as the method is known, was often used for early products made from cellulose-nitrate sheet and postwar products made from acrylic sheet.

Early blow-moulding techniques used air to form hollow mouldings, by inflating two sheets of thermoplastic material softened by heat and clamped between hollow moulds. Today the method uses extruded tube, which is clamped and blown in a mould in a similar way.

Hollow mouldings may also be produced by coating a heated mould with a polymer paste. This latter method, known as slush moulding, is used for making flexible dolls and low-cost squeaky toys.

Extruded thermoplastics are produced by forcing the heated raw material through a shaped die and then cooling it. This method is used for making continuous lengths of a specific profile.

Compression moulding uses powdered thermosetting material to fill the mould – which is then heated until the plastic flows, whereupon the mould is fully compressed. On curing, the mould is opened and the plastic moulding removed.

Injection moulding usually uses granules of thermoplastic material fed by hopper into a heated chamber; when molten, the plastic is injected under pressure into a sealed mould.

Lines left in the surface of the plastic often distinguish moulded objects from ones that have been fabricated by machine – the lines indicate where the mould was split in order to remove the finished article. With injection moulding, there is also a circular mark where the plastic was introduced into the mould.

Shellac

More commonly known as a finish for fine furniture, shellac was also used – with the addition of organic fillers such as wood flour, or powdered minerals such as slate dust – to make a compression-mouldable thermoplastic. The material was capable of being moulded with fine detail and made into items such as boxes and photo frames. Perhaps the most common example is the 78 rpm gramophone record.

This form of plastic is a relatively brittle material and will distort if subjected to excessive heat. Melted shellac has the smell of sealing wax. When shellac records were superseded by ones made of vinyl, some of the old records were handcrafted into decorative bowls or pots by softening in hot water.

To clean shellac plastics, remove surface dust with a soft brush and wipe with a soft cloth dampened with a warm, mild liquid-soap solution.

Cellulose nitrate

Cellulose nitrate was developed in the mid nineteenth century as collodion for coating photographic plates and as a treatment for wounds. From this it was developed as a plastic material (called Parkesine) by Alexander Parkes and first shown at the International Exhibition in 1862. It was later developed in America as celluloid, and in Britain as Xylonite. It is an important material, for cellulose nitrate was the first synthetic plastic to be manufactured from natural polymers. A variety of domestic items and playthings, as well as early cine film, were made from it. Many of these products were postformed or blow-moulded from precut sheet material made in a wide range of colours. Initially celluloid was produced to imitate ivory and tortoiseshell. When it is warmed, you can detect a cellulose-nitrate plastic by the distinct smell of camphor, which was used as a plasticizer during its manufacture.

Caring for celluloid
Celluloid is highly flammable and should not be exposed to a naked flame – nor kept in a humid environment, as that will accelerate its deterioration. Store pieces in a dry, relatively cool atmosphere on open shelves or in a ventilated cabinet and out of direct sunlight. Do not seal pieces in plastic bags.

If the surface shows signs of deterioration such as blooming or fine crazing below the surface, seek the services of a plastics conservator, as it may be possible to halt the damage. As decaying celluloid can infect other pieces close to it, remove the offending article from your collection and store it elsewhere. It may even become necessary to dispose of the decaying article.

Clean sound pieces with a warm, mild liquid-soap solution applied with cotton-wool swabs or a soft cloth – but first carefully remove any old wax or greasy deposits with paraffin. Dry with an absorbent paper tissue. Do not apply a surface finish to the cleaned plastic.

Hard rubber

Vulcanite or ebonite, as it is also known, is a hard-rubber material that came into existence around 1839, although it was not produced commercially until the middle of the nineteenth century. Originally it was made by vulcanizing natural rubber, but it was also produced using synthetic rubber when this became available in the 1940s.

Moulded into a variety of small objects, including buttons, combs, jewellery and fountain pens, typically vulcanite was black – but it was also produced in a pink colour for making dentures, as well as brown and a striated mixture of black and red.

Vulcanite is susceptible to light and heat, which causes the surface to oxidize and take on a dull greenish-brown hue. If, after handling the material, your fingers have a sulphurous odour it indicates that the object is made from a hard-rubber compound. When vulcanite degrades, sulphuric acid is released and, if the plastic is wetted, it can form marks known as 'water spotting'. Always wear cotton gloves when handling old pieces, to avoid moist hands transferring sulphuric-acid contaminants from one piece to another, leaving fingermarks. Handle the material as little as possible.

Caring for vulcanite
Keep vulcanized-rubber articles in low light and in cool, dry conditions. Clean the surface with a soft cloth dampened with a light mineral oil, or apply a thin covering of microcrystalline wax. Buff with a clean soft cloth.

Casein

Casein is produced from the protein found in cow's milk. At the end of the nineteenth century it was found that casein treated with formaldehyde formed a moderately water-resistant, translucent, thermosetting plastic. This was produced in a wide range of colours, and also used to imitate natural materials such as tortoiseshell and horn.

Most items made from casein – such as fountain pens, belt buckles and hand brushes and hand mirrors, as well as the more common decorative buttons – are fabricated from solid sections and not usually moulded.

Caring for casein

Casein will give up and absorb moisture, which can result in fine crazing of the surface. Keep articles in a moderate, stable environment and out of direct sunlight. Clean with swabs of very mild liquid-soap solution, then blot dry with absorbent tissue. First test the surface to establish if the colours are fast. If they are not, work on a small area at a time. Seal the surface with a fine film of microcrystalline wax.

Cellulose acetate

Cellulose acetate is based on the same natural polymer as cellulose nitrate, but uses acetic acid to produce a non-flammable thermoplastic. Its initial applications were similar to celluloid but, with the development of suitable plasticizers in the early part of the twentieth century, it began to be used for the newly developing injection-moulding processes.

A tough material, it is widely used for toys in preference to brittle materials such as Bakelite or polystyrene.

When cellulose acetate degrades, it displays signs of white blooming or distortion. It also gives off the vinegary smell of acetic acid. Treat products made from cellulose acetate as you would celluloid. However, as some have volatile plasticizers that tend to evaporate, causing the object to distort, keep them in a closed, unvented cabinet.

Thermosetting plastics

These are produced as powders for moulding into rigid household wares and fittings by the application of heat and pressure. Bakelite is arguably the most familiar brand name of this type and was to epitomize the new era of mass-produced plastics. Developed in 1909 in the USA, by L.H. Baekeland, a Belgian-American, it was the first solely synthetic-resin plastic. Formed from phenol (a derivative of tar or benzene) and formaldehyde and combined with fillers, it made a hard, stable, strong plastic with excellent electrical and heat-resistant properties.

Bakelite was used for a wide range of domestic products in the electrical-appliance field, particularly moulded radio and television cabinets. Most were a dark-brown colour, and some were mottled. A casting type of phenol-formaldehyde resin was also produced in translucent form and a range of colours.

Caring for Bakelite

Sunlight can cause the surface to dull and loose some colour, but otherwise the material is not unduly harmed by normal domestic conditions. Clean with a mild liquid-soap solution applied with a soft cloth, but do not soak in water. Dry with a soft clean cloth. If you want to revive the colour, use a mildly abrasive car-paint cleaner applied with a cloth pad, then wash the plastic again. Protect the surface with a fine coating of microcrystalline wax, as appropriate.

Amino plastics

This is the technical term for a range of thermosetting resins based on urea and its derivatives combined with formaldehyde. Although produced and used in a similar way to phenolic resins (see above), they were made in a wide range of light and dark colours.

The first – marketed under the name Beatl, derived from 'Beat All', an advertising slogan – was introduced in the mid 1920s. Urea-formaldehyde and melamine-formaldehyde resins followed, the latter in the mid 1930s. Both were rigid and strong, but melamine had the advantage of having improved scratch and heat resistance. Melamine is commonly used for tough, colourful tableware, as well as plastic laminates for work surfaces. Care for amino plastics as for Bakelite (see above).

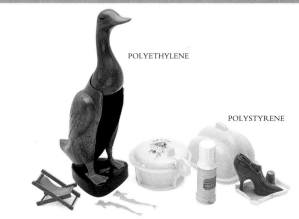

POLYETHYLENE

POLYSTYRENE

Polyvinyl chloride (PVC)

PVC is a synthetic thermoplastic material produced by polymerizing vinyl chloride. It is a relatively rigid plastic that can be modified by the use of plasticizers to make a flexible material, and by other additives for use in a variety of ways.

The early PVCs of the 1930s were relatively unstable and were produced in film form and as flexible sheet material. Later PVC was combined with fabric to make leathercloth, and moulded to make flexible toys such as soft-faced dolls and squeaky playthings. Its low cost and ability to be moulded with fine detail enabled it to become the preferred material for making recording discs.

Modern rigid unplasticized PVC – the development of which began in the 1950s – is now a common material used by the building trade for items, such as window frames and claddings, that were formerly made from wood.

Caring for PVC
Old PVC products are likely to lose their flexibility due to a loss of plasticizer. Do not flex hardened-plastic items unduly. Keep them out of direct sunlight and in a cool environment. PVC plasticizer may affect other plastics: it will dissolve polystyrene items in contact with it, so store them in separate compartments. Clean dirty surfaces with a mild liquid-soap solution, then dry with a soft cloth. Do not use solvents on plasticized PVC.

PVC

ACRYLIC RESIN

Acrylic-resin plastic

Polymethyl methacrylate, commonly known as Perspex or Plexiglas, is a water-white transparent thermoplastic. Typically produced in sheet or rod form, it is made in a wide range of translucent and opaque colours.

A liquid resin for cold casting is also produced and may be recognized by its use for decorative pieces featuring embedded objects, although in recent times polyester resin has been the preferred material for this purpose.

Developed in the 1930s, sheet acrylic was widely used as a substitute for glass. It was also formed and machined into a variety of domestic items. It can be solvent welded and hand polished, and is readily worked by ordinary handtools and machine processes. Mouldable acrylics were also made, and were used for such items as buttons and telephone appliances in place of the older Bakelite versions.

AMINO PLASTICS

Caring for acrylic plastic
Perspex is a stable plastic that weathers well. Clean with a mild liquid-soap solution, then pat dry with an absorbent cloth or tissue. Do not rub the surface, as this causes a static charge that will attract dust. However, anti-static cleaners (available from specialist suppliers) provide a protective coating that lasts for a month or more. Avoid the use of solvent cleaners, as these can cause crazing of the polished surface.

The high-gloss surface will readily scratch if abraded, so remove surface dust regularly with a soft brush. Fine scratches can be polished out relatively easily (see page 136).

Polyethylene

Polyethylene – or polythene, as it is more commonly called – is a thermoplastic and was first produced in 1933. Derived from ethylene, it is a tough, flexible, waterproof, highly insulative, acid-resistant and non-toxic plastic. It is made in two basic versions: low-density (which has a soft greasy feel) and high-density (which is more rigid). It has a translucent grey-blue colouring, but is also made in a range of opaque and translucent colours. Typical uses include food containers, toys, and novel and decorative household wares.

Polystyrene

Polystyrene is a hard, rigid, somewhat brittle, transparent thermoplastic, made in a wide range of colours. Produced in quantity in the latter half of the 1930s, it has excellent moulding and insulative properties. High-impact grades were introduced in the late 1940s, although they have since been superseded by the modern ABS plastics; they are typically found in opaque colours.

Polystyrene can be injection moulded, thermoformed and extruded. It can also be bonded with a solvent adhesive. It has been widely used in the manufacture of electrical appliances, household wares and toys, and in recent years as foamed insulants and packaging. You can usually identify polystyrene by the tinny metallic sound it makes when tapped.

Caring for polyethylene and polystyrene
Protect old examples from strong light, as these plastics are liable to degrade and their colours fade. Clean with a warm, mild liquid-soap solution. Do not use solvents for cleaning polystyrene.

REPAIRING PLASTIC ARTEFACTS

Generally plastics are not easy materials to work, making attempts at repair difficult. Most plastic artefacts are moulded in one piece – but some have separate moulded or fabricated components that are assembled with mechanical fixings such as self-tapping screws, and others may be bonded together.

Most plastics do not glue well, although both thermosets and rigid thermoplastics can usually be bonded with epoxy-resin adhesive. Cyanoacrylate glue can also be used for small repairs – although conservators tend not to use it, as the long-term effect of its solvents are not yet known.

Polystyrene and acrylic plastic can be glued with their own solvent adhesive. Polystyrene cement (commonly used for plastic kits) is available from model shops, and acrylic adhesive from suppliers of acrylic plastics. These will produce a strong weld-like bond, but need to be applied carefully to avoid damaging the surrounding plastic.

Stress cracking

Stress in plastic can be recognized as a light bloom on some plastics and fine crazing in the case of acrylic and polystyrene plastics, an effect that is compounded in the presence of solvents and bonding cements. In severe cases it causes the plastic to break. Stresses can be caused by the moulding process, applied pressure or heat generated by fabrication processes. Manufacturers of acrylic try to overcome stress problems by a controlled heating and cooling process.

Little can be done once stress damage occurs – but as a general rule, to avoid accelerating the problem, do not use solvents to clean plastics. However, lighter fluid or paraffin can be used sparingly to remove sticky gum deposits from all plastics other than rigid polystyrene, acrylics and flexible PVC.

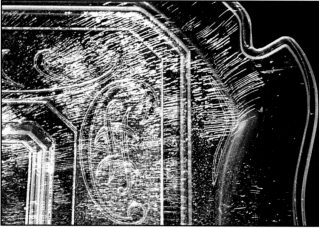

Mending broken Bakelite

Being relatively brittle, Bakelite is easily broken if struck or dropped. Mouldings are usually made with thick walls, enabling the broken edges to be aligned and bonded together in a similar way to ceramics. If necessary, use lighter fluid to remove greasy deposits from an old break, then wash the plastic with a warm, liquid-soap solution.

1 Applying glue
Assemble the break without glue to check the fit. Heat the parts slowly with a hair dryer until the plastic is hot to the touch. This will encourage the glue to flow in the joint. Apply a thin film of epoxy-resin adhesive, prepared according to the manufacturer's instructions, to the broken edge of the main component. Fit and press home the broken-off piece. Apply strips of self-adhesive tape under tension across the break to hold it together until the glue sets.

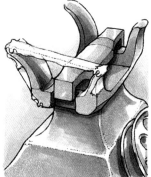

2 Trimming the joint
Before the glue is fully cured, peel off the tape and, using the tip of a scalpel, carefully slice off excess glue from the break. To avoid marking the polished surface, don't let the blade dig into or scrape the plastic.

3 Filling chipped edges
If necessary after gluing, fill a chipped edge with a coloured filler made from ground-up scraps of Bakelite mixed with epoxy-resin adhesive. Clean up the filled surface with a knife, as described above.

Removing scratches

Acrylic plastics (Perspex) have a high-gloss surface that can be marred by scratches. It is possible to remove deep scratches by hand, using fine water-lubricated wet-and-dry abrasive paper followed by hand polishing (see below). However, it is much easier to use a power buff fitted with a calico mop treated with a mildly abrasive buffing soap. Use only light pressure, to avoid overheating the plastic. Work a larger patch than just the scratch area, to 'feather' the edge in order to avoid obvious distortion in the surface.

Polishing by hand
A matt surface resulting from fine scratches can be polished out by hand, using proprietary acrylic polishes available from plastics suppliers. Alternatively, use a mildly abrasive chrome-polishing cream.

Apply the polish with a soft cloth pad, working in an overlapping circular motion. Finally, buff the surface with a clean soft cloth.

IDENTIFICATION OF PLASTICS MATERIALS

MATERIAL POPULAR NAME	COLOUR	CLARITY	CHARACTERISTICS	FORM	TYPICAL EXAMPLES
HARD RUBBER VULCANITE EBONITE	Typically black, but also red and ripple mixtures.	Opaque.	Hard. Gives off sulphurous smell if rubbed. Turns brown when exposed to light.	Machine fabricated or moulded.	Vesta boxes, combs, fountain pens and jewellery. Pink vulcanite was used for dentures.
SHELLAC FLORENCE COMPOUND	Dark brown, black, or red ochre.	Opaque.	Hard and brittle. Smells of sealing wax if melted.	Usually moulded.	Decorative picture frames, 78 rpm records, boxes and union cases.
CELLULOSE NITRATE CELLULOID XYLONITE	Any colour, including mottles, pearls and special effects.	Transparent, translucent or opaque.	Flexible and tough. Smells of camphor when warmed by rubbing or warm water.	Usually very thin sheet. Hollow mouldings may be filled with plaster to add weight.	Thin covering on mirror backs and other dressing-table items. Fountain pens.
CASEIN ERINOID GALALITH	Any colour, including mottles, pearls and special effects.	Usually opaque, but some translucency when used for mock tortoiseshell and horn.	Hard. Sometimes smells of formaldehyde when placed in water.	Usually machined to shape, sometimes hot-stamped into shallow shapes. Not moulded.	Coloured knitting needles, buttons and propelling pencils.
PHENOLIC MOULDING POWDER BAKELITE	Usually brown, red, or green mottle, or plain black or brown.	Opaque.	Hard and brittle. The surface is often discoloured brown and will mark a tissue rubbed against it. May smell of carbolic when warmed.	Always moulded to shape.	Radio cabinets, ashtrays and electrical plugs and sockets.
CAST PHENOLIC RESIN CATALIN	Any colour is possible, but rarely white or blue.	Often translucent and marbled, seldom transparent and sometimes opaque.	Hard. The surface is often discoloured brown and will mark a tissue rubbed against it. May smell of carbolic when warmed.	Usually cut sections of rod, tube etc. Often carved.	Animal napkin rings and carved bangles. Also 'Carvacraft' deskware and some American radio cabinets.
AMINO PLASTICS BEATL BANDALASTA LINGA-LONGA BEETLEWARE MELAMINE	Any plain colour, but also marbled or speckled.	Never transparent, but can be translucent and sometimes marbled like alabaster. Beetleware may be translucent or opaque. Melamine is opaque.	Hard and brittle like Bakelite, but amino plastics do not discolour with age.	Always moulded to shape.	Bandalasta and Linga-longa: colourful, marbled picnic ware. Beetleware: pale-coloured electrical plugs and sockets. Melamine: tough, colourful tableware.
CELLULOSE ACETATE ACETATE BEXOID	Any colour, usually plain, but occasionally marbled.	Transparent, translucent or opaque.	Tough and slightly soft, may be flexible in thin sections. Often smells of vinegar, especially when warmed.	Normally moulded.	Films, some spectacle frames, 'Pedigree' dolls and some toys.
ACRYLIC RESIN PERSPEX PLEXIGLAS	Any colour, but pastel colours were popular.	Transparent, translucent or opaque.	Hard, not brittle. Smooth glasslike surface that is easily scratched.	Normally fabricated by hot-shaping from sheet, but can also be moulded.	Shallow dishes, lamps, clocks, and transparent brooches with carving on rear.
POLYVINYL CHLORIDE PVC VINYL	Any colour.	Transparent, translucent or opaque.	Soft and very flexible, though modern PVCs can be rigid and tough. Surface may feel 'tacky'.	Leathercloth coatings or moulded.	Flexible 'squeaky' toys, hollow balls, fashion belts and gramophone records.
POLYSTYRENE STYRENE	Any colour. Pearl was popular for a while, as were 'streaky' colour effects.	Transparent, translucent or opaque.	Hard and brittle, but sometimes toughened. Very 'tinny' metallic ring when tapped.	Usually moulded.	Toys, self-assembly models, and cheap 'give-aways'.
POLYETHYLENE POLYTHENE ALKATHENE	Any colour.	Generally translucent, but sometimes opaque.	Soft and flexible. Has greasy feel and can be scratched with fingernail.	Usually moulded.	Air-tight food containers, toys and 'poppit-bead' necklaces.

GLOSSARY

Where they differ,
American terms appear in
bold italics after their British
equivalents.

Acetone
Colourless flammable liquid used
as a solvent and cleaning fluid.

Acid-free
Term used to describe a material
(usually paper or cardboard
manufactured from rag fibre or
purified wood pulp) that has a
neutral or slightly alkaline pH
factor.

Acrylic varnish
Clear water-based varnish, used
primarily as a wood finish or as a
protective coating for paintings.
It is also used to simulate glaze
when restoring ceramics.

Airbrush
Designed to spray paint and
other finishes such as glaze or
varnish, an airbrush is capable of
extremely precise work.

Alloy
A mixture of two or more
metals.

Animal glue
Traditional woodworking
adhesive made from animal skin
and bones. It is supplied in the
form of granules or gel for
mixing with hot water.

Banding
Plain or patterned strip of veneer
used to make decorative borders.
See also cross banding.

Black-lead polish
Oil dressing
A mixture of graphite and soft
waxes that produces a dark-grey
metallic sheen on cast iron.
Manufactured originally as a
grate polish.

Blister
Small raised area of veneer
resulting from insufficient glue at
that point.

Block
The core of a bound book,
comprising leaves of paper sewn
and glued together.

Bloom
Cloudy white stain that appears
on clear finishes affected by the
ingress of moisture or by the
application of heat.

Blueing
The controlled production of a
protective film of rich-blue oxide
that prevents steel corroding.
Blueing is used extensively for
gun barrels and for the hands of
clocks and watches.

Bodying up
The process of applying
successive layers of shellac polish
(French polish) to create a film of
the required thickness.

Bolt ring
Hollow circular clasp,
incorporating a retractable bolt,
used as a fastening for bracelets
and necklaces.

Boulle
Decorative inlay comprising
sheet brass and tortoiseshell. Also
known as buhl.

Bradawl
Small handtool for boring holes.
It has a sharp screwdriver-like
tip that severs the grain,
preventing the wood splitting as
the tool is inserted.

Britannia metal
A form of pewter, containing tin,
antimony and copper. It is
stronger and lighter in colour
than 'old' pewter and is often
used for electroplated metalware.

Brushing French polish
Shellac polish formulated for
application with a paintbrush
instead of the usual cloth pad.

Buffer
An alkaline substance added to
card or paper to ensure they are
acid-free.

Button polish
Superior-quality French polish
made nowadays from golden-
brown shellac flakes.

Cabochon
Domed unfaceted stone set into a
piece of jewellery.

Came
Grooved strip of lead used to
hold the quarries in place in a
leaded light or stained-glass
window. *See also* quarries

Carat
Unit used to measure the purity
of precious metals and the weight
of gemstones.

Cellulose filler
Spackle
Water-based filler used by
decorators to patch holes or
cracks in plaster. Can also be
used as a filler for restoring
damaged earthenware.

Chamois leather
Soft suede polishing cloth made
from goatskin or sheepskin, also
known as a shammy or chammy
leather. It was formerly made
from the hide of a chamois
antelope.

Close grain
Term used to describe fine-
textured wood with small closely
spaced cells.

Closed setting
Metal mounting with an
enclosed recess for a gemstone.

Crackle glaze
Glaze that is deliberately crazed
during the manufacturing process
to create a decorative finish for
some ceramics.

Crazing
Fine network of cracks found in
the glaze of pottery or porcelain.

Cross banding
Strips of decorative veneer
banding with the grain running
at right angles to the main axis.

Cut glass
Glassware decorated with facets,
deep grooves and hollows cut by
an abrasive wheel.

Cyanoacrylate glue
Clear general-purpose adhesive
with an acrylate base. Known
commercially as 'superglue'.

Distilled water
Water that has been distilled
commercially to remove
impurities.

Document cleaner
Powdered eraser contained in an
open-weave bag, used for
cleaning soiled paper by gentle
abrasion of the surface.

Document-repair tape
Self-adhesive, acid-free paper
tape made with reversible acrylic
adhesive.

Dust jacket
Removable printed-paper sleeve
wrapped around a bound book.

Earthenware
Opaque porous pottery, fired at
a relatively low temperature, that
requires the application of a glaze
to make it waterproof.
Earthenware has a comparatively
thick coarse-textured body and
comes in a variety of colours,
ranging from reddish brown to
off-white and black.

Ebonized
Stained black to imitate genuine
ebony.

Ebony polish
Black-stained French polish used
for finishing very dark woods.
Ebony polish was traditionally
the preferred finish for pianos.

Electroplating
The process of applying a thin
coating of metal, such as silver or
chromium, onto a base metal by
means of electrolysis.

Enamel
Coloured opaque or translucent glass fused to a metal base. Intricate patterns are formed by different methods. With cloisonné enamelware, for example, the areas of colour are separated by flattened metal wire soldered to the base. The base itself is engraved for champlevé enamelling, and the resulting hollows are filled with enamel.

Endpaper
The sheet of paper glued to the inside of the board cover at the front and back of a bound book. One half of the endpaper forms the flyleaf.

Epergne
Ornamental centrepiece for a table. Usually designed to hold flowers or fruit.

Ephemera
Collectable items, such as tickets, labels and posters, originally not intended to last for more than a short time.

EPNS
Electroplated nickel silver. *See also* nickel silver.

Epoxy glue
Two-part adhesive comprising an epoxy resin and a hardener. When the two are mixed together, the resulting chemical reaction produces a strong, insoluble bond.

Epoxy putty
A two-part filler or modelling compound that sets hard when the two components are kneaded together.

Faïence
Tin-glazed earthenware.

Feathering
The action of creating an indiscernible edge to a coat of paint or varnish by blending it into the background colour.

Figure
The pattern of grain on the surface of a piece of solid wood or veneer.

Flats
Short for flat figures. Flats are usually cast-metal model soldiers in low-relief, about 1 to 2mm (⅟₁₆in) thick.

Flux
Substance used to clean the surfaces of metals prior to soldering.

Flyleaf
The free half of an endpaper. The first and the last leaf of a bound book are flyleaves.

Folder
Narrow bone spatula used by bookbinders to rub sharp creases in folded paper. Also used for burnishing down adhesive tapes and glued paper.

Foxing
Small brown spots caused by spores growing on the surface of damp paper.

Frass
Fine wood dust created by the activity of wood-boring insects.

French polish
Wood finish made by dissolving shellac in alcohol, applied with a pad of wadding wrapped in cotton or linen cloth. *See also* brushing French polish, button polish, ebony polish, garnet polish, transparent polish, white polish.

Fumed silica
Finely powdered silica used as a matting agent.

Garnet polish
Deep red-brown French polish, sometimes used to enhance the colour of mahogany and similar woods.

Gelatine
Fine powder prepared by boiling specially prepared animal skin and bones. When mixed with water, gelatine is an excellent paper size.

German silver
See nickel silver.

Gesso
Paste made from rabbit-skin glue and chalk. When applied to wood, it can be sanded to a smooth base for gilding with gold leaf. Coloured gesso is sometimes called bole.

Gilding
The process for applying gold leaf or gilt varnish.

Glaze
Hard, glassy transparent coating applied to ceramics, to make them waterproof and for decorative purposes.

Glue starvation
Describes a condition where insufficient glue has been applied to veneer groundwork or woodworking joints, resulting in a breakdown of the bond.

Gold leaf
Wafer-thin sheets of pure gold applied to a surface as a decorative finish. Metal leaf, made from brass, is a cheap substitute.

Grain
The general direction or arrangement of the fibrous material in wood. *or* The direction of the warp and weft threads in woven textiles.

Grain filler
Thin paste used to fill the open pores of wood prior to applying a glossy wood finish, such as French polish.

Groundwork
The backing material, either solid wood or man-made boards, to which veneers are applied.

Hairline crack
Barely visible crack in porcelain or earthenware.

Hard-paste porcelain
A mixture of kaolin (china clay) and petuntse (china stone), hard-paste porcelain originated in China around 900 AD. Bone china, made with animal-bone ash, is the standard English and American hard-paste porcelain.

Hard-solder
To make a strong joint between two metal surfaces by fusing a layer of brass or a high-melt solder between them. The process is also known as brazing.

Headband
Narrow cloth band attached to the top and sometimes also to the bottom of the spine of a book.

Hinges
See joints.

Hydrogen peroxide
Bleaching agent available in volume strengths.

Hygroscopic
Having a tendency to absorb moisture from the air.

Inlay
To insert pieces of wood, metal or semi-precious materials into prepared recesses, so that the materials lie flush with the surrounding surfaces. *or* The piece of inlaid wood, metal or semi-precious material.

Intaglio
Incised carving in the surface of a stone or seal.

Japanning
Glossy finish in imitation of Oriental lacquer.

Joints
The two hinges between a book block and its board covers, formed by a strip of mull reinforced with tapes and covered by the endpapers.

Jump ring
Openable metal link at each end of a chain for attaching a clasp or bolt ring.

Key
To abrade or incise a surface to provide a better grip when gluing something to it or in order to create a strong bond between the surface and a finish such as paint or varnish.

Kilim
Woven rug with no pile, manufactured mainly in the Middle East.

Laying off
Using upward strokes of the brush to blend in the wet edges when finishing an application of paint or varnish.

Leaded light
Window panel made from quarries (small pieces of clear, coloured or textured glass) held in a matrix of narrow lead strips known as cames.

Lime scale
White deposit of mineral salts contained in hard water.

Lipping
Protective strip of solid wood applied to the edge of a panel or table top.

Lot
Single item or group of items offered for sale at an auction.

Lustre glazes
Metallic finishes for ceramics produced by adding appropriate salts to the glaze.

Lustres
Drop-shaped pieces of glass or crystal hung from chandeliers, lamps and candlesticks to reflect the light.

Man-made boards
Stable panels manufactured from veneer or wood particles bonded together under pressure.

Marquetry
Relatively small pieces of veneer laid together to make decorative motifs or patterns. *See also* parquetry.

Masking tape
Low-tack self-adhesive tape used primarily to mask and protect areas surrounding surfaces that are to be painted.

Mazac
Alloy of magnesium and zinc used for making die-cast toys.

Methylated spirit
Denatured alcohol
Alcohol that has been denatured by the addition of methanol and pyradine. Often coloured with a violet dye, it is used as a solvent, thinner and cleaning agent. Commonly known as meths.

Microcrystalline wax
Light, white wax polish used as a dressing for a variety of materials.

Mull
Light open-weave muslin fabric glued to the inner spine of the binding of a book. It forms a major component of the joints between the book block and board covers.

Nacre
Mother-of-pearl. The hard iridescent substance that forms the inner layer of certain mollusc shells.

Nickel silver
Nickel silver, an alloy of copper, zinc and nickel also known as German silver, is used as the base for plated silverware marked EPNS (electroplated nickel silver).

Niello
Decorative technique for metalware. It consists of a black compound of silver and sulphur with lead or copper, fused into an incised design or pattern.

Open setting
Metal mounting that holds a gemstone in place, but which is open at the back to admit light.

Ormolu
Gilded cast bronze or brass, used for ornaments and for decorative mounts applied to furniture, clocks and sometimes ceramics.

Oxalic acid
Toxic crystalline dicarboxylic acid, used as a bleaching agent.

Paraffin
Kerosene
Thin fuel oil distilled from petroleum, used as a solvent and cleaning agent.

Parian ware
White unglazed porcelain, often used for figurines because of its resemblance to marble.

Parquetry
A process similar to marquetry, but using veneers cut into geometric shapes to make decorative patterns.

Patina
Surface colouring and texture produced by a combination of natural ageing and long-term use.

Pile
Texture produced by the cut ends of knotted yarns used to make rugs and carpets.

Pinchbeck
Named after its creator Christopher Pinchbeck, an eighteenth-century watchmaker, this alloy of zinc and copper was made to imitate gold. Used for cheap jewellery, it had gone out of fashion by the mid nineteenth century.

Planish
To produce a finished surface on metalwork by light hammering.

Plate
An individual printed picture used as a book illustration.

Plating
See electroplating.

Polyethylene
Polymerized ethylene resin used to manufacture protective sheeting and packaging. Commonly known as polythene.

Porcelain
The fine, white vitrified body of porcelain is created by high-temperature firing. It is extremely hard yet translucent. *See also* hard-paste porcelain and soft-paste porcelain.

PVA adhesive
White glue
Ready-mixed water-based woodworking glue. A conservation grade is used by bookbinders for repairing books.

Quarries
The individual pieces of glass in leaded lights and stained-glass windows.

Restringing
The process of replacing a worn or broken necklace thread.

Reversible
Describes a process that can be undone easily and which does not have a lasting effect on the piece being worked on.

Rivet
Metal staple used for reinforcing repaired ceramics.

Rubber
Polishing pad
Soft pad used for applying French polish, made from a handful of cotton wadding wrapped in a square of linen or cotton cloth.

Sealer coat
An application of diluted finish applied to bare wood to prevent subsequent full-strength coats soaking in.

Section
Part of a bound book comprising a single sheet of paper folded, trimmed and sewn to create a number of individual leaves.

Sgraffito
Form of decoration used on ceramics. Sgraffito is created by scratching through the slip to expose the ceramic body beneath.

Sheffield plate
Thin rolled-sheet material consisting of silver fused to a copper backing. One or both sides may be plated.

Shell chip
Small semi-circular chip, a common defect on the rim of cups, plates, vases and other ceramic items.

Shellac
Derived from the resin excreted by the insect *Laccifer lacca*, shellac is dissolved in industrial alcohol to make French polish. Shellac has many other uses, including the production of sanding sealer and sealing wax.

Short grain
Describes where the general direction of wood fibres lies across a narrow section of timber.

Silicon-carbide paper
Sandpaper manufactured from grains of black to dark-grey silicon-carbide attached to a paper backing with waterproof glue. Known as wet-and-dry paper, it is used with water as a lubricant for rubbing down coats of paint or varnish. A pale-grey silicon-carbide paper coated with a dry powdered lubricant is used for rubbing down finishes that would be harmed by water.

Silver cloth
Polishing cloth impregnated with non-abrasive metal polish for cleaning silverware.

Silver gilt
Silver covered with a thin film of gold.

Slip
Clay mixed with water to a creamy consistency, used for decorating ceramic pieces.

Soft-paste porcelain
With its slightly granular texture, soft-paste porcelain was the result of early European attempts to copy Chinese porcelain.

Soft-solder
To join two metal surfaces together using low-melt solder applied with a heated soldering iron.

Soumak *See* sumak.

Spelter
Alloy of copper and zinc used for decorative wares and as a substitute for bronze in the manufacture of cast statues.

Spine
The bound edge of a book.

Sprue
Waste plastic or metal that solidifies in the access channels in casting moulds.

Stained glass
Leaded lights containing painted-glass quarries.

Stainless steel
Relatively modern silver-coloured, rust-resistant alloy of steel and chromium.

Stake
Stout piece of wood or metal bar used to back up a workpiece when shaping or planishing metalware.

Stoneware
Hard ceramic with a coarse granular texture, made by adding flint or stone dust to the clay. Increasing the temperature of the kiln fuses the body and glaze, making it non-porous and harder than low-fired earthenware. Stoneware is usually white, light-brown or beige in colour. Black basalt ware and blue jasper ware are exceptions.

Stove-enamelling glaze
Transparent glaze that sets in a relatively low temperature in a domestic oven. It is specially formulated for recoating restored ceramics.

Straightedge
Strip of metal or wood machined with at least one true edge, used to mark and cut straight lines and to gauge flat surfaces.

Stringing
A narrow strip of wood used to divide areas of veneer.

Sumak
Type of flat-woven rug from the Caucasus and northwest Persia.

Tacking iron
Thermostatically controlled tool with an electrically heated tip. Used by paper conservators and bookbinders to apply heat-set tissue (tissue paper coated with dry adhesive).

Tarnished
Lightly corroded.

Thinner
Substance used to reduce the consistency of paint, varnish or polish.

Tinning
Coating the tip of a soldering iron with molten solder.

Tinplate
Thin rolled-steel sheet plated on both sides with tin.

Tipped in
Lightly glued into a book.

Titanium dioxide
White pigment used as an additive in glue to reduce its tendency to yellow.

Transparent polish
Practically clear French polish that hardly changes the natural colour of wood.

Turpentine
Short for spirits of turpentine. A colourless oily liquid with a pungent odour, used as a solvent for paint and varnish.

Veneer
Thin slice of wood used as a surface covering on less costly materials, such as pine or man-made boards.

Veneer hammer
Tool with a narrow brass strip mounted in its head, used to apply firm pressure when gluing veneer by hand.

Verdigris
Green deposit on brass, copper or bronze produced by corrosion.

Warp
The longitudinal foundation threads of a woven fabric. *or* To twist or cause to twist out of shape as a result of damp or heat.

Water stain
Grey or brown stain caused by moisture drawing dirt and other impurities into the fibres of cloth or paper.

Weft
The transverse threads of woven fabric. Weft threads weave over and under warp threads.

Weld
To fuse together two pieces of metal or plastic by the application of heat or pressure. When welding metal, it is normal to apply additional molten metal to the joint. With plastic, a solvent is often applied to the joining surface.

Wet-and-dry paper
See silicon-carbide paper.

White polish
Milky-white variety of French polish made from bleached shellac. It is used for finishing pale-coloured woods.

White spirit
Mineral spirits
Colourless solvent obtained from petroleum, used as a thinner for paints and varnishes. Also known as turpentine substitute.

Window mount
Piece of card with a rectangular aperture, commonly used when framing pictures behind glass.

Wire wool
Steel wool
Mass of fine steel strands, used for smoothing surfaces and applying finishes.

Woodworm
Larvae of the furniture beetle that feed on wood fibres, leaving an intricate network of fine tunnels in the timber.

Index